MASH UP!

HOW TO USE YOUR MULTIPLE SKILLS TO GIVE YOU AN EDGE, EARN MORE MONEY AND BE HAPPIER

IAN SANDERS & DAVID SLOLY

KoganPage

LONDON PHILADELPHIA NEW DELHI

First published in Great Britain and the United States in 2012 by Kogan Page Limited

120 Pentonville Road	1518 Walnut Street, Suite 1100	4737/23 Ansari Road
London N1 9JN	Philadelphia PA 19102	Daryaganj
United Kingdom	USA	New Delhi 110002
www.koganpage.com		India

© Ian Sanders and David Sloly, 2012

The right of Ian Sanders and David Sloly to be identified as the author of this work has been asserted by them in accordance with the Copyright, Designs and Patents Act 1988.

ISBN   978 0 7494 6590 2
E-ISBN   978 0 7494 6591 9

British Library Cataloguing-in-Publication Data

A CIP record for this book is available from the British Library.

Library of Congress Cataloging-in-Publication Data

Sanders, Ian, 1968–
    Mash-up! : how to use your multiple skills to give you an edge, earn more money and be happier / Ian Sanders, David Sloly.
        p. cm.
    Includes index.
    ISBN 978-0-7494-6590-2 – ISBN 978-0-7494-6591-9   1. Career development.
2. Vocational qualifications.   3. Job satisfaction.   I. Sloly, David.   II. Title.
    HF5381.S269 2012
    650.1–dc23
                                                        2012011859

Typeset by Graphicraft Limited, Hong Kong
Printed and bound in India by Replika Press Pvt Ltd

Contents

Acknowledgements

→ Thanks to everyone who spoke to us for the book.

→ To the Mash Bunch: Alexia Leachman, Austin Kleon, Dave Shields, Dave Stewart, David Hieatt, Frances Booth, Jose Castillo, Kevin Roberts, Mark Hillary, Melissa Pierce, Paul Benney, Sarah Graham, Sejal Parekh, Shane Mac, Steph Booth, Steve Sampson and Zoë Howe.

→ To the people we sat down with who shared their insights: Julia Hobsbawm, Phill Jupitus, Terrence Watts and Tom Hulme.

→ To the other people we spoke to whose stories and experiences we've shared in these pages: Gary Vaynerchuk, Harry Drnec, Jamie Klingler, Martha Lane Fox, Matt Flack, Michael Mentessi, Mike Southon, Raj Dey and Sarah Beeny.

→ To the places that accommodated us on our journey: the Bull Hotel, Bridport and the Hive Beach Café, Dorset where we started; the wonderful staff of the Square Bar, Bristol; Elisa and Ash at the Coffee Bean Company in Leigh-on-Sea; and all those other coffee shops that kept us stimulated in between.

→ The amazing Liz Gooster for her help and support.

→ To Zoë Sanders for the illustrations.

→ To Dave Shields for the photo of Ian.

→ Ian would like to thank his wife Zoë for not only totally getting what he does, but also supporting him in all he does. And to her, Barney and Dylan for letting him spend weekends writing books.

→ David would like to thank Annette and Hunter Sloly for their love, food and smiles.

→ Three things we couldn't have written this book without:

- coffee;
- Google Docs;
- giant beanbags.

About the authors

Picture credit: Dave Shields

Ian Sanders is passionate about capturing and communicating ideas. He works with businesses to turn their thinking into marketing content that tells a story across multiple platforms. His career has been an obsession with 'doing', driven by curiosity and insight rather than a big plan. Ian applies a rapid mindset to all projects, recognizing that the value lies in execution. Through his own ideas and writing he's on a mission to disrupt the business status quo. His books have inspired readers to change their lives; Tom Watson, the British MP who famously challenged Rupert Murdoch, said "Thanks Ian. You helped me rediscover the inner rebel."

David Sloly originally trained as a journalist with the BBC and at the end of his course he humiliated a politician and was promptly fired. He was soon snapped up to create leftfield content for the UK's first independent radio production company. He went on to produce creative work for radio and TV before moving into advertising and then on to marketing where, as creative director he dreamt up award-winning campaigns for some of the world's biggest brands. David is a partner at Prime-Decision, an independent company founded in 2011 which offers behavioural insight and strategy. He is also a hypnotherapist, so if an employer tries to fire him again, he simply hypnotises them into drastically increasing his salary. David lives in Bristol with his wife and son.

Introduction

So does this sound familiar? Throughout your life, you've been forced to make black or white choices, the results of which placed you in a very defined box, with a neat little label on it. You were One Thing or Another.

A teacher didn't suggest you mixed up a load of random subjects; she suggested you specialize in one area: the arts or sciences. Probably not arts and sciences. Your first job specification probably wasn't 'We're not sure what this role is but you'll be doing a bunch of useful stuff.' It was probably clearly defined. A fixed role or discipline. A specialism perhaps. Clearly defined. Black or white.

The trouble with a black and white world is that it misses the glorious spectrum of technicolour that sits in between. That kind of delineation may be great in theory, on an organizational chart or in a linear career trajectory, but reality tells us there is a disconnection between this single-specialism focus and how people really, truly are.

This book is about exploring the interesting areas in between the black and the white. It will show you how the areas in between can make a real difference in your life, giving you both a career edge and greater fulfilment.

So stop dismissing all these wonderful opportunities in your life and start embracing them. After all, you're probably more adept than you think at dealing with plurality. You probably do it all the time... without thinking about it. You watch TV and browse Facebook. You probably have 12 tabs open on your web browser. You're good at switching from one thing to another... just like that. Now it's time to scale up.

In pursuit of writing this book we've been on a journey, talking to mashers around the world. From London to Austin, Texas, Sao Paulo to Switzerland, we've been hearing stories from workers who do more than one thing. We've heard from artists, photographers and comedians, as well as designers, executives, writers and innovators.

We got some interesting answers. One person told us they did not agree with our theory. Well, hands up: we don't have a theory. This is not about a fixed strategy to working plurally. We don't have a doctrine or an ideology; we're just interested in what it is that makes people do more than one thing, whether it's economic circumstances, a pushy boss, deep desires or, more likely, just things happening by accident. We were fascinated by hearing these stories. We've connected the dots with our own experiences and created this book – a guidebook to making the most of this mashed-up world.

If you're wondering why these two guys are qualified to help you on your journey, read on...

THE STORY OF HOW I GOT HERE
by David

I can recall as a child my father changing his job. My parents came into the living room and announced it to me one afternoon. I cried. I was too young to know that I was supposed to be happy, so this unexpected change that interrupted my playing with toy cars and was delivered with such seriousness didn't feel like a celebration. That was the only time in my memory that my father changed his job. Once in my living memory. Now as I look at my own boy, too young to understand much beyond the toy cars that occupy his time, I wonder, how many jobs will I have before he leaves school? And if he cries every time I change my role he is going to be one teary little chap.

Now as I stand at the train station on a damp Tuesday morning waiting for the 7.30 am heading to town to meet Ian, I fish out my mobile phone from my pocket and scan through the detail of the meeting we are heading to. I call up the profiles of the people we will be presenting to and in my mind run through what I believe will be the defining thinking that will secure me another revenue stream. I litter the thinking with my relevant past experience that qualifies us for the job – a job that just five years ago did not exist, which prompts me to wonder, what will I be selling myself as in five years from now? How many other roles will I have pitched myself for between waiting for this train and five years' time? What new skills will I have learnt to ensure I stay employable?

THE STORY OF HOW I GOT HERE
by Ian

I guess I always liked the idea of mashing-up interests. As a kid I saw that our hobbies and passions were plural, not singular; I bought records by The Jam *and* Joni Mitchell; no one said you have to choose between Lego and Meccano. So why did the teacher tell me I had to choose Art *or* Politics when it came to making subject choices? That never worked for me. When I failed to get a place at university, 1986–87 became the year I went plural: taking Photography and Film Studies courses at the local college; working at a music distribution company; and working at the local BBC radio station. It combined all my interests in music, broadcasting and the arts in a veritable 'Celebrations' pack of delights! That pattern repeated itself 10 years later when I worked at Unique Broadcasting, inventing my own unique role, 'Special Projects Director', which swept different roles across the group. The 1986 accidental mash-up set the precedent for a life in organizations and working for myself, where I have always mashed up things. Why? Because I'm curious and love exploring new things. Also because I get bored easily and need new stuff to touch. And also because I like to think I'm good at more than one thing. And I know that gives me a competitive edge where I can offer clients and the job market more than one thing. It may scare the heck out of some people, but it's how I love to work.

TALES OF THE MULTIDIMENSIONAL

Four mashers tell us why they mash

As with many career decisions, there are different reasons people go plural. Sometimes it's out of a premeditated plan to carve out a new work life; other times it's out of necessity to create revenue or to keep a job. So, to kick things off, here are four short tales illustrating some catalysts for change. We hope their words will inspire you to put some mash into your life.

Julia's story

Julia Hobsbawm is founder and CEO of Editorial Intelligence, a media networking business. She's London's first Professor of Public Relations at the University of the Arts, and a visiting Professor of Networking at Cass Business School. She sits on the World Economic Forum's Global Agenda Council and is a prolific writer, speaker and commentator on communications, entrepreneurship and work–life balance. She is a Strategic Adviser to the global communications firm Edelman and runs worklifeseesaw.com which provides coaching and mentoring about work issues. Her current work life is a result of her following a cluster of interests, and creating opportunities off the back of them:

❝ I think people should always just follow both their interests and what they're good at, and 90 per cent of the time what they're good at does correlate with their interest. There is no grand strategy. I don't think life is like that. I think you can be strategic in saying 'No' to things.

On the day we met, she was profiled in a double-page spread in London's *Evening Standard*, a photograph of her annotated with scribbled headings of the different areas she covers: Media, Law, Women, Business, PR, Academia, Politics, Charity.

❝ People who sit well in the mash-up environment instinctively know what they feel comfortable with; they don't have to plot it empirically.

Austin Kleon's story

Austin's story is a tale of a guy crossing borders from web design to copywriting. Having studied art and writing in college, he got a job as a librarian teaching senior citizens how to use computers. Austin decided to use his design skills to make better websites so people wouldn't need librarians to teach them how to use them. This gave him the ability to handle both design and copywriting, but in marketing agencies, an area he was looking to work in, those two roles are normally separated. Austin broke the mould and is now considered an asset: he's the copywriter who delivers the art and design too, making him highly employable. We first became aware of Austin's work through his blog post 'Steal like an artist', which has since spawned a book of the same name.

I got tired of designing pretty websites that didn't say anything, so I decided to move over to [copywriting].

Phill's story

Phill Jupitus's career over the past 25 years has been a true mash-up: starting out as a performance poet, working for a record company, being a stand-up, TV performer, presenter, panellist, actor, musician, cartoonist, writer, podcaster and broadcaster. But he's probably best known for comedy, whether appearing on BBC radio panel shows or as a panellist on the long-running BBC2 music quiz *Never Mind the Buzzcocks*. His story of going plural is about being true to all he does, exploring a number of opportunities that came off the back of being a stand-up. Phill loves the freedom of plurality, the TV show has given him the financial stability to build a portfolio around, and he can now seek other opportunities and gigs that appeal to him, however random they may seem.

It's never been about a plan and it never will be. As soon as you start having a plan... it goes wrong.

David's story

David Hieatt was the founder of howies (with a small 'h'), the sportswear company he sold to Timberland. With his book publishing business, jeans company and restaurant concept and as founder and curator of the Do Lectures, David is a great example of a masher. But ironically he only went plural because of a non-compete clause stating he couldn't start another clothing business. So David put all his energies into creating – and curating – the Do Lectures, an annual ideas festival in Wales, starting a pub and restaurant with a friend and finally, when the non-compete clause ran out, setting up a jeans company too. He acknowledges it was a random process.

❝ So plural came about from a non-compete clause in a contract. I will let you know if that was a good thing or not...

'WORK' USED TO BE SO SINGLE-TRACK. PICK A TRADE AND CLIMB A LADDER. KEEP CLIMBING; DON'T STOP.

First there was sausage...

It's easy to forget how things were,
so let's remind ourselves...

'Work' used to be so single-track. Pick a
trade and climb a ladder. Keep climbing;
don't stop; and, whatever you do, don't
even think about changing your trade;
that would surely show you as weak.
So we became mechanics, bankers,
designers. We were expert at One Thing
and One Thing Only. The mash-up world
is about a plural, multidimensional
approach to work, perfecting multiple
skills that reflect our multiple talents.
You don't need to be a freelancer to live
the mashed-up life – mashing is
a portable mindset that you can take
and apply to your work life to create
fulfilment or inject into your
organization to create a more
innovative business.

Right now, more than ever in the history of the human race, the world is your oyster. You can change tack, mash things up, learn a new skill and apply it for money. Plurality will not dilute your career success or organizational efficiency; it will enhance it. Today, the notion of being defined by a single job title alone is antiquated, the kind of idea you'll see in a glass case in a museum: that is *so* 20th century. In this century, no one knows what's around the corner, but there is one known truth: there is no such thing as a job for life any more. Success in this new world of work will be about delivering value by staying adaptable. But, as we know, it wasn't always this way...

Historically, we came from folk working the land, with a sprinkle of blacksmiths, carpenters and potters. We produced pretty much just what the collective would require to survive. The blacksmith made the horseshoe and fitted it, the carpenter designed the chair, fabricated it and sold it, and the potter did similarly. No factory, no production line, no supply chain. Then in the 18th century something happened in the United Kingdom that would spread to the rest of the world and have a profound effect: the Industrial Revolution arrived and with it came economic change. We no longer just produced enough to sustain our life; we set out on a path of sustained growth. Factories sprang up and mass production began. New jobs that had previously been unimaginable suddenly needed filling, and new skills had to be learnt. A man – for it usually was a man – would feel certain he would work at this place for his life, only to be replaced by his son when he was too old to pull the lever. That much was certain.

Now we are in the middle of a new revolution, and the certainty that our children will be inheriting our jobs is as far-fetched as the adventures of *Alice in Wonderland*.

As for now? Our global economy, blindsided in 2007, shudders under the weight of uncertainty, reminding us that what appears stable today can collapse whilst we sleep at night. Entire countries go bankrupt, and the world prints so much money to plug the gaps that you would require the entire floor space of the world's IKEA stores to house it all. Yet from these ashes opportunity appears at an almost equally fantastical rate. If someone had told you 20 years ago that you would be standing on a train platform with a phone that enabled you to see on a screen where a plane overhead had come from and was heading to, you would have been spellbound. Yet here we are, in the midst of the greatest revolution of them all. Decoding the building blocks of life, sharing intelligence in an instant, growing in labs the very stuff that makes us human.

We live in a world that is creating, connecting and communicating, but that has very little certainty. To stay in employment, grow our businesses or secure the next contract we need to be open to change, able and willing to learn new skills, and alert to see when those skills resonate together, creating a new one. We also need to be accepting that certainty is a word to be used sparingly.

❝❝ In the real future you will be working at a stint rather than a job. To work at a stint is to become part of a project team for 18 months, followed by joining three friends doing a start-up business that folds after two years, after which you sign on with a multinational which disappears in a merger... and the beat goes on.

(Hiemstra, 2011)

Today fewer people are in jobs. This trend doesn't mean we are sitting on our collective backsides watching daytime TV and eating Doritos. It means more of us are doing our own thing, carving out work lives that transcend a single job.

So now we have an opportunity. Amongst all that uncertainty, amidst that doom and gloom, there is the power in the mash-up thinker. Whether you work for yourself, a small business or a global corporation, the masher knows how to spot an opportunity and use it to make a difference, to build a reputation – to really stand out. Mashers are not just the free-lancers picking up ever more complex projects. They're the CEOs who are launching new ventures and the staff juggling multiple roles. They've become distinctive for all the right reasons. They're the ones who get that promotion, get that dream job in Hong Kong or, yes, even survive not being placed on the 'under consideration for redundancy' list. They're the ones who are putting up their hands and saying 'I can do that.'

New job titles are appearing all the time. These are not just recycled old titles updated to be more attractive to talent; these are roles that demand new skills that simply did not exist ten, five or even two years ago. As fast as one door closes another one opens. The advance in technology is creating new positions demanding new skills everywhere, not just online. So as a workforce we benefit from being able to pivot quickly, understanding and appreciating all our skills and being ready, willing and excited to walk into a new workspace and deliver on a new project. It is up to you to decide what skills you can add to complement the ones you already have and to apply them to your job or business.

Standing still is not an option. Understanding what you will need to do to meet your inner desires is an option. Following your passions is an option. There is no time for doomers and gloomers of the popular press, if you want the edge, money and happiness you have to take the responsibility for your life back. You will need to focus on what you want and tune out those with old-fashioned outlooks to the new world we are approaching.

'What do you want to be when you grow up?' A sentence our children around the world are being naively asked by teachers, friends and parents. It reflects society's obsession with the singular. Not only is our world demanding we prepare for change but it doesn't seem natural to do just one thing any more, does it? We want to be good at lots of things. Currently our education forces us to stay singular by asking the dreaded 'What do you want to be when you grow up?' question. It asks this question because it has always asked this question.

A friend's 14-year-old niece was asked by her teacher what she wanted to be when she finished school. The teacher asked her to think hard about it and then get back to him with an answer. She didn't know what to say to her teacher. A friend, on hearing the girl's predicament, said: 'Tell your teacher that, perhaps, the thing you want to be when you leave school hasn't been invented yet.'

Just 10 years ago Facebook, eBay and LinkedIn did not exist. You simply could not order your weekly shop online for delivery at 8.30 on a Sunday evening. Five years ago Twitter did not exist and you could not tap an app on your phone and fling some Angry Birds whilst heading to your job as a Content Manager. Here are five jobs, fuelled mainly by technology, that if your teacher had asked you what you wanted to be when you grew up you probably wouldn't have given as an answer:

→ **Blogger.** Yes, people are blogging full time and earning a very good living at it too. The more people you have reading your blog the more valuable you are to advertisers.

→ **Social Media Strategist.** Someone has to figure out what you should be saying and where you should be saying it.

→ **Smartphone App Developer.** Changing our world one tap at a time, app developers are in demand. App designers, work flow managers, mobile content specialists and soon 3D experts will be in great demand for mobile.

→ **Information Architect.** An entire business moves online. How will people find what they want? How will information link? An Information Architect looks at logic and connections that ensure the end user gets the right stuff at the right time.

→ **Corporate Social Responsibility Manager.** Once upon a time a big green bin sat in the corner of the office and on occasion the caring bespectacled quiet member of staff could be seen throwing paper in it. Now prospects want to know details of your corporation's responsibility programme before they allow you to tender.

But of course it's not just the emergence of new roles; the revolution has changed how and where we work. For the digital nomads – people like your authors – the technological revolution has enabled us to run our businesses from coffee shops and co-working spaces. Who needs a flash office any more? We don't. That flatter internet world has lowered the traditional barriers to entry for people starting businesses. Since you can get a website started for the cost of a domain name, you can start trading in an instant. So, for the mashed-up thinkers, we *can* run businesses from home. We *can* trade goods with people all over the world. We *can* life-coach by Skype, with clients in every corner of the world paying their bills via PayPal. This means that, despite the doom and gloom and all that talk of economic collapse, the ability to start a hobby business or a business on the side has mushroomed. The tools for this new business life? A mobile phone, good ideas and a contact book. How cool is that?

So press pause and start rethinking your work life right now. Whether it is inspired by the emerging roles we have just described or the opportunities of launching a web-based business, there need be no limits to your imagination. You want to mix being a part-time civil servant with teaching yoga and being a freelance photographer? Do it. You're an HR manager, but want to launch a web-based business selling kids' clothes on the side? Go for it. Want to be an author and a therapist and instruct people in ballroom dancing? Why not? In fact we'll meet that guy in the next chapter.

Name: Dave Stewart

Location: Los Angeles

Twitter: @davestewart

Twitter Bio: "Likes To Do Things"

Although you might not guess it from his enigmatic Twitter bio, Dave leads a very multidimensional work life. Best remembered as one half of the Eurythmics, Dave is a prolific Grammy award-winning musician and producer working with the likes of Bob Dylan and Bono. But he's also an author, entrepreneur, film-maker and philanthropist. His company Weapons of Mass Entertainment is an 'ideas factory' based in Los Angeles that develops projects in film, television, publishing and music.

1   **So tell us your multidimensional talents, how you earn a living.** I'm an ideas person and I have built a company employing brilliant talented people who 'get' my ideas and know how to make their part work.

2   **When did you transition to go plural, to be more than 'just' a musician?** Around 1982 I started shooting film and taking photos, etc.

3   **What's your strategy for answering the 'What do you do?' dinner party/pub question (if people don't know the full range of your talents)?** A Cultural Engineer.

4   **How do you communicate/sell your multidimensional talents?** I make actual physical or digital things that demonstrate what it is or could be that I'm selling. That along with my vision.

5   **What are the joys of a work life where you mash up different talents?** Never bored, endless stream of possibilities, meet new people, always celebrating.

6   **And what are your pain points in doing more than one thing?** Very tiring sometimes. Usually once a month I get exhausted.

WELCOME TO THE WONDERFUL WORLD OF MASH, A WORLD WHERE YOUR WORK LIFE CAN REFLECT YOUR MULTI-DIMENSIONAL TALENTS.

...and then
there was mash

In the wonderful world of mash, people no longer have just one core skill to offer; they have two, three or more. We are chefs, mixing up different tastes and ingredients to create a compelling dish. By themselves the constituent parts may sound odd, but mixing them together can gain you a Michelin star. In this workplace mash-up the smart people are creating new revenue streams with each skill they add, at the same time making themselves highly employable and carving out more authentic work lives. Organizations are also seeing the benefit of mashed-up roles where productivity and innovation soar. So it's goodbye to the sausage factory and welcome to the wonderful world of mash.

Mashing is not some crazy left-field idea practised by the few. Mashers are everywhere. In your street, on your train carriage, in your local coffee shop. Thousands of us are choosing to create multidimensional work lives and exploding the myth that you must be defined by a single job title alone.

So many career paths are dictated by the label around your neck. In the world of the creative industries – where both of us have spent most of our working lives – you were a Creative (a producer, a designer), a Suit (an account director, a new business person) or a Geek (a web developer, an engineer). And traditionally you wouldn't see many people mash up these disciplines. But there's no reason why you can't. Now we are seeing the emergence of people who have 'crossed borders' from one discipline to another, and of roles that mix up previously segmented skills. When we both started our careers in broadcasting we were told we had to make a clear black or white choice: did we want to be a creative or a manager? How flawed is that thinking? Why can't people cross borders from one thing to another? Who says they have to stay in that pigeon-holed box all their career? Why can't a designer also be good at spreadsheets? After all, in this world full of data we need people who can bring information to life – a designer who can present financial data in a beautiful way is quite an asset. That crossing of borders is our own story. David's been a creative director at an ad agency; he's also a hypnotherapist and started out as a journalist. So David's experience has given him a toolbox with three drawers: journalism, hypnotherapy and creativity. Each one of those drawers had a whole bunch of tools that collectively he can use to fix many things. David did not strategize for reinventing himself from journalist to creative director; he just broke the rules and crossed the borders.

David's desire to do this was not born out of breaking the rules for the sake of it, but to carve his own unique work life, to hack the perfect career for himself. You can do this yourself: to create a work life that transcends the singular, that goes beyond fixed titles and labels without fear of having to follow any rules about what you can and can't do.

When we think back to our parents' careers we usually see a linear, one-dimensional journey. A job for life was a real possibility, so people stuck with that, happy to be in work, and the job title provided an identity, a sense of definition, a means of providing confidence and self-assurance. Leonardo da Vinci was a painter, sculptor, architect, geologist, cartographer, botanist, musician, scientist, engineer, inventor, anatomist, mathematician, writer, designer, innovator, architect and technician. His curiosity knew no boundaries, so he was able to explore everything and anything that interested him.

Thinking of ourselves as the next Leonardo may seem a little far-fetched, because you'd imagine surely the guy must have never slept to achieve all this? In fact historians tell us that even Leonardo suffered from procrastination. Yet he still managed to acquire so many skills that his business card would have needed to be the size of *The Last Supper* to fit them all on. So don't limit your thinking; lots of people today are carrying around multiple job titles and they're comfortable with it.

The misconception about plurality is that, if you are adept at doing more than one thing, it must dilute your abilities to be good at any one of them. But generalists and specialists are not mutually exclusive; David knows his stuff in the therapy room as well as in the creative studio – he's got that depth but in more than one discipline. What drives that breadth is a curiosity to get involved in multiple disciplines and projects, exploring new ideas. Kevin Roberts is CEO Worldwide of Saatchi & Saatchi, one of the world's largest creative organizations. He sees the value of this breadth:

This whole notion of specialization versus generalization I believe is a crock. It limits people. In my experience, people are much more capable than their specialty might suggest. Indeed to only focus on specialization leaves a good deal of man's potential unrealized.

Tom Hulme, Design Director at global innovation firm IDEO, looks at this slightly differently. Rather than think about it as a division between generalism and specialism, he talks about the themes of exploration and exploitation. In simple terms, every aspect of every organization can be split into 'exploitation' and 'exploration'. The specialists are exploiting opportunities, whilst the mashers are out exploring, discovering the next big opportunity. The mashers have the mindset to cross borders and apply learnings from one area to another. The value is that businesses and consumers receive better new products and services from this exploration. Tom observes:

> ❚❚ **The consumer doesn't care. The consumer is totally agnostic to however a company structures itself; they just see an offer that cuts across [everything].**

Every business needs the explorer who represents the customer, and it is the masher who best fills this role. Mashers are able to cut across all the silos and figure out what is required next. This is valuable for organizations that want to maintain a competitive edge.

Some people may recoil in horror at the thought of being multidimensional, so we sought the help of Terence Watts to explain the personality types that best fit plural working.

Terence is one of the UK's most respected practitioners and teachers of hypnotherapy, and is the author of *Warriors, Settlers and Nomads: Discovering Who We Are and What We Can Be.* Of course Terence is mashing on the side (because he likes to keep busy) as a professional ballroom and Latin American dancer, who until recently had been running his own school. *Warriors, Settlers and Nomads* has been described as a handbook for understanding your personality. The book brings to life the truths of our character types: the warrior, the settler and the nomad. Each type has unique skills and attributes that make them better at certain aspects of life. Terence explains that these are the three key influences on our behaviour and that in order to be happy and successful we must understand our dominant character and adhere to it. He warns of the danger of trying to kid yourself that it can be any other way. So let's look at the three personality types:

1 **The warrior** is determined and goal orientated, with an ability to bring plans to fruition. Warriors are natural team leaders and great coordinators who remain calm in emergencies. They are logical and quite practical, but they do need to be in control. Is this you?

2 **The settler** is sociable and gets on well with most people. Settlers tend to be adaptable to situations, possess great communication skills and therefore be quite persuasive and confident. They have a high level of instinct and general awareness. The Achilles heel is that they need to be liked. Does that sound like you?

3 **The nomad** personality type likes to live a busy life with something going on all the time, so constant stimulation is a must. Nomads are outgoing and have a built-in enthusiasm for new projects, especially those that include communication, such as presentation, publicity and promotion. They are confident and lively and can inspire and uplift others, but they do require lots of stimulation.

Not many people can put themselves in just one category. We tend to be a mix of two or three. You may lean heavily towards the settler with a little nomad, or see the warrior in yourself but with some settler too. So how does that translate to your ability to deliver on a plural work life?

Well, warriors tend to lack flexibility but are able to stay on track, whereas settlers tend to lack staying power but are adaptable to situations, and nomads tend to get bored easily but can turn their hand to many different things.

If you are a warrior and settler mix then it will mean that you are not particularly flexible, and staying power may be an issue. If you are the settler with nomad then you will certainly be interested in the new, but will you have the staying power to deliver it? If on the other hand you are the nomad type with some warrior then congratulations. The advantage of the nomad and warrior is that you can turn your hand to many different areas, especially if it is new or modern; and the warrior will combat the nomad's tendency to become easily bored and in danger of losing focus.

It's important that you feel comfortable delivering on many different projects if you want to embark on a life of mashing roles, so being clear that you are the kind of person who will feel confident doing that is important. It simply is not for everyone, but by the very fact you have this book in your hands you are probably of the right mindset to live the plural life.

Name: Kevin Roberts

Location: New York and New Zealand

Bio: CEO Worldwide, Saatchi & Saatchi

1   **So remind us of your multidimensional working life; what are the roles you execute in addition to being CEO?** Chairman of USA Rugby; Founding Partner of Inspire, a leadership consulting company; Board Member of NZ Telecom; Trustee of TYLA (Turn Your Life Around Trust); Founding Partner of Red Honey Cosmetics, a four-store cosmetic retail operation in New Zealand; Teaching Professor at Auckland and Lancaster universities.

2   **When did you transition to go plural?** Ten years ago.

3   **What's your strategy for answering the 'What do you do?' dinner party question?** My one word equity is 'inspirational'. I try to make the world a better place by inspiring others to be successful in business... I believe we live in the Age of the Idea and that it is the unmeasurable power of creativity that will accelerate progress.

4   **How do you communicate/'sell' your multidimensional talents?** By blogging, speaking and doing.

5   **What are the joys of a work life where you mash up different talents?** Constant learning, responsibility and recognition.

6   **And what are your pain points in doing more than one thing?** None. The gods first make bored those whom they wish to destroy!

HOW ADOPTING A MASH-UP
WAY OF WORKING WILL
MAKE YOU AN ASSET TO
EMPLOYERS.

Using mash as a competitive edge in the job market

The job market is uncertain and is likely to remain that way for some time.

So how can adopting a mash-up way of working help you and your business? By having multiple tools and talents to offer an employer you will be viewed as an asset. We have spoken to organizations that not only encourage plurality in their workforce but actually depend on it!

In many organizations the idea that you have a single job role is fast becoming outdated. There are three key drivers creating this change. The first is that staff are being asked to perform more than one role or cross borders to mix two previously siloed disciplines. Secondly, in some organizations staff are being encouraged to invent their own job specs, creating unique roles that are a net result of their desires and talents. And finally your multidimensional role may be a sign of the times; is your employer asking you to take more on as redundancies are made around you?

Rather than people joining organizations and having tightly defined job titles, many roles are being defined by the person filling them, and as a result recruiters are not interested just in depth of specialism any more; they're also interested in your breadth. Previously organizations advertised that they needed certain roles filled, inviting applications from candidates who were specialists in that area. Often, hirers did not even pay attention to other passions and talents outside of the job spec. Now we're seeing that changing. The way this is best demonstrated is in small businesses, where there are fewer rules and fixed job specs. New people arrive and carve out their own role. Certainly, they have a responsibility as the Salesperson or the Engineer, but they are able to add value in multiple ways beyond that, which could never have been displayed in a job ad.

There is a new recognized power in the multi-skilled in larger organizations too, where workers can create fame and fortune for both themselves and the employer. Would you rather be Employee number 14, an executive in the marketing team of a corporation, or Marketing Exec and Social Media Star in the same organization? What's more distinctive? What stands out from the crowd? What's the better story to tell at the job interview? 'I'm a successful marketing exec' or 'I'm a marketing exec who's made a name for myself getting results from social media'? What brings more fame and fortune?

We've picked the social media example for a good reason. In 2012, organizations are still struggling with social media. Until recently the world's biggest grocery brand did not know how to use Twitter. Meantime the 20-year-old dude working at the skater shop is proficient. So he becomes more than just the shop assistant; he's the Twitter guy. He makes his boss's skater shop so good on Twitter that it becomes the go-to store for miles around, and online too. The dude has no paper qualifications, no MBA; he just learnt it, as 'digital natives' do. It was second nature; his knowledge became powerful. If you happen to know stacks about social media, or how to write copy for online, or are a good storyteller, then you can try mashing that up with your day job to create a truly authentic, multidimensional offering. Whether you are the social media star in the marketing department or the Twitter dude in the skate store, not only are you creating a job that is more fulfilling and a true reflection of who you are, but by default you are creating a great career stepping stone. Mashers who were smart enough to spot a vacuum and fill it have instantly created a stronger, more compelling narrative to communicate their value at job interviews, appraisals and in job applications. The successful masher does not wait for permission or consent to become multidimensional. The masher is the person who sticks her hand up at that company meeting saying, 'Yes, I want to do it.' She is the one who responds instantly and thoughtfully to a tweet and turns a potentially negative situation into a positive one. She is the one who approaches the boss volunteering to take an additional area of responsibility. It may only pay kudos rather than cash in the short term, but in the long term it will make you more distinctive and much more employable. It's a fact of life that many in junior positions are well aware of.

Interns and entry-level roles often get experience of working in different departments, across separate disciplines. The advantage is that they get a good understanding of other parts of the business; regardless of where they end up they have empathy for other aspects, roles and disciplines. The irony is that these starters have an advantage over more senior people who get so entrenched in the organizational silos. A friend of ours works in an organization where the people in the sales department always have their doors closed and don't mix with others. This is not unusual and creates problems. It needs the mash-up worker to bridge some of these divisions, to bring in some mash diplomacy that can create a more productive organization rather than one that deals with interrelationships through 'them and us'.

Cristina Pansolini, an entry-level employee at the ad agency Saatchi & Saatchi in New York, explained online how she effectively has three roles and no fixed job title:

❝❝ I work in the Internal Communications Department, in the Social and Emerging Media Department, and in the Strategic Planning Department. I'm very much an entry level employee, and don't have an official title. I appreciate Saatchi letting me have a hand in different departments so I can choose which direction I really want to go into.

(Pansolini, 2012)

Having three roles at the start of her career means Cristina has learnt to be a pluralist at an early stage, adept at juggling more than one role or discipline that will be a great asset throughout her career. It gives her more variety and arguably a more stimulating job, whilst giving great value to her employer. As she says, this breadth means she can try her hand at a number of different areas before having to choose where – and indeed if – to specialize. And of course, regardless of where she ends up, she will have that all-important empathy and understanding for other bits of the business. Saatchi & Saatchi are not alone; other organizations are encouraging it too. IDEO is a global design and innovation company; the company's CEO, Tim Brown, introduced the theme of T-shaped people back in 2005. What are T-shaped people?

❝ They have a principal skill that describes the vertical leg of the T – they're mechanical engineers or industrial designers. But they are so empathetic that they can branch out into other skills, such as anthropology, and do them as well.

(Brown, 2007)

According to recent research, employers are struggling to find enough of these people. Being T-shaped allows people to explore insights from different perspectives and recognize patterns of behaviour that yield ideas. Having those T-shaped people enables IDEO to look for broader solutions; a client company comes to them when it doesn't have the answers itself, and by definition they're usually excellent at seeking answers internally from their own specialists. The T-shaped people have that breadth as well as the depth, able to look for inspiration outside the normal field. Ben Malbon, Executive Director of Innovation at the ad agency BBH New York, has made the case for the digital advertising industry also needing more T-shaped people. In a 2010 presentation Ben argued that, as what they as an agency produce has evolved, then so how they produce it needs also to evolve:

❝ We need people fluent in at least one language. But literate in many.

(Malbon, 2010)

That multi-literacy can make people more innovative. We spent an afternoon with IDEO Design Director Tom Hulme and learnt how they rely on plurality to be innovative and effective to their clients. Tom believes that plurality is the trait of creativity:

> Taking inspiration from loads of eclectic places enables our people, individually or in teams, to genuinely come up with new ideas. And that's what our clients hire us for.

After all, their clients don't tend to hire IDEO for what they're already great at. Tom went on to add:

> We depend on that plurality. If you're not self starting and entrepreneurial [here], you can get quite lost because it's not formulaic; we don't have constrained job descriptions that create a balanced scorecard of performance. So people tend to have to carve out their own roles, carve out their own careers.

So organizations like IDEO are looking for 'idea fusers', those people who have that breadth of skills and experiences to blend one discipline with another to create those game-changing ideas.

So let's look at where a new role has arisen after two disciplines became mashed together. Edward Boches, Chief Innovation Officer at the ad agency Mullen, has talked about the emergence of a new role, the Creative Technologist, mashing together creativity and technology:

A creative technologist can teach people about digital tools and platforms and how to create with them. Good ones can inspire writers, designers and even creative directors with possibilities they may never have imagined. A few of the best might even be able to transform a company, affecting the work, the teams, and the processes necessary to keep up with all the change and the opportunities that technology constantly presents.

(Boches, 2011)

If you're reading this thinking your industry or business is immune from the emergence of brand new roles like this and that the idea of mashed-up roles is purely head-in-the-clouds stuff, then think again. Mashed-up nine-to-five roles are not just for the creatives in ad agencies and innovation businesses. There are examples of people mashing much straighter disciplines like finance or HR. Meet Jamie Klingler. Jamie is currently Publishing Manager at ShortList Media, the business that publishes the weekly magazines *ShortList* and *Stylist*. Jamie's previous job at ShortList? She was Editorial Finance Manager and Photography Director at the magazine publisher, doing those two jobs at the same time, juggling spreadsheets with choosing images for the magazines. Jamie was not setting out to explode any myths for the sake of it; as the business was fairly small when she joined, the combined role happened organically. Her job before joining the magazine had been in a sales position selling photography, so she was quite used to handling financials and budgets. Jamie told us how this mashed-up approach aided each respective job:

> **I think that the budget/finance perspective definitely made me better as a photo director, as I was able to see where we were spending and what value that was delivering to readers, which made a lot of difference as to where we were spending.**

Also not only did having that plural role make her job more varied, but it actually led to her current Publishing Manager role being created, so she was able to continue carving out her own destiny.

In the way that people are mashing multiple disciplines, so some people are mashing multiple businesses. A few years ago, the idea of a senior manager running more than one business may have seemed crazy. Today in Silicon Valley there are many examples of CEOs running more than one business. Jack Dorsey is one of the founders of Twitter. He is currently CEO of mobile payments platform Square as well as executive chairman of Twitter. At the 2011 Techonomy conference in Tucson, Jack laid out his strategy for mashing two roles: it's all about theming his days. Each day, he focuses on one specific aspect of corporate development and tunes out the rest. He explained the way he segments his working week:

Monday: Management meetings and 'running the company' work;
Tuesday: Product development;
Wednesday: Marketing, communications and growth;
Thursday: Developers and partnerships;
Friday: The company and its culture.
He told the conference 'There's interruptions all the time, but I can quickly deal with an interruption and know "it's Tuesday, I have product meetings, I have to focus on product stuff," he said. "It sets a good cadence for the company."'

(money.cnn.com)

So whether you're a CEO running more than one business or the junior starting out in your career, plurality is not just an abstract concept – it's a reality within your grasp. Now is the time to think about establishing your plurality as a competitive edge in the job market – it clearly is a real asset that employers are attracted by.

Name: David Shields

Location: Leigh-on-Sea, England

Bio: Photographer, arts event organizer, shop assistant

1 **So tell us your multidimensional talents, how you earn a living.** Photographer in fine art, travel and people (weddings is a speciality). Partner in events company Beach Hut Events specializing in art, craft and design shows. Part-time assistant in the camera shop Jessops. Also a part-time stop-at-home dad.

2 **When did you transition to go plural?** All started back in 2003 when I started working for myself.

3 **What's your strategy for answering the 'What do you do?' dinner party/pub question?** Tend to stick to 'Photographer'; if they are still interested will mention the other strings to my bow.

4 **How do you sell your multidimensional talents?** I am passionate about *all* that I do. I don't think there is any need to sell when your passion comes through. I thrive on the positive response from people when things go right!

5 **What are the joys of a work life where you mash up different talents?** Each day is different. I could not be a nine-to-fiver! Plus as I work from home I can work in the evening (when my creative juices flow best). This gives me more time to spend with my young son, giving me that more fulfilled life we are all looking for.

6 **And what are your pain points in doing more than one thing?** I have to say there are no pain points. I love working for myself, plus I am lucky, as all my titles/jobs are linked together. I am either taking photographs, selling them, helping other people sell theirs or being a house husband/stay-at-home dad – which includes taking many photos of my son!

HOW YOUR PERSONAL
UNIFIER WILL SHOW
THE WORLD THAT YOU ARE
SO MUCH MORE THAN
A JOB TITLE.

04

Your personal unifier

It's probably OK that your father-in-law can't articulate what you do, but it is not OK if people you meet through your business networks don't understand what you do, because if they don't get it you won't be working with them.
In the old world a job title would have done this for you, but in the mashed-up world a title will just not cut it. Why? Because you are not your job title; you are so many more things than that, and that means it's more difficult to communicate. To overcome this, you'll need a personal unifier.

'What do you do?' is a familiar question to all of us. And it's not always an easy one to answer.

A personal unifier will give your answer clarity and make your plurality gettable. So together let's work out your unifier so you can easily share your talents with the outside world and at the same time have a set of criteria for checking that everything you do fits. Both of us love the variety and randomness of all we do, but we still like giving it some clarity. The unifier does that.

Here's how to find your unifier. Let's take Ian – he needed to find the common denominator that bound together all the things he offered. Here is how he did it. He started by listing all his different offerings, not by job title but by short description in a list. Under each he put three thoughts that described the value of what he offered. So it looked something like this:

Ian

1 Writing and blogging:

- generating ideas;
- interviewing entrepreneurs;
- telling compelling stories.

2 Thought leadership marketing:

- understanding the business;
- creating content;
- communicating ideas.

3 Helping companies communicate their ideas:

- understanding, distilling and simplifying business ideas;
- finding the best platforms to communicate them;
- creating content to communicate those ideas.

Then he selected the single most important thought from each category and crossed out the other two thoughts. He was left with the following:

1 Telling compelling stories.

2 Communicating ideas.

3 Understanding, distilling and simplifying business ideas.

One common denominator is that Ian tells stories. But when you tell someone you're a storyteller it gives the wrong impression. So it immediately fails the 'What do you do?' test; storytelling is the wrong unifier. But something else stood out here: *Ian communicates ideas for clients.* He does this by telling stories, simplifying the complex and communicating ideas to a wider audience. So he landed on a simple unifier: 'I communicate ideas.' It passes the 'What do you do?' test, as it does not create the wrong mental picture and opens the conversation. Now it became much easier to get through those initial introductions. A unifier makes the complicated simple. It helps others understand you and it helps you understand yourself, so when you are thinking of adding another skill to your list you can ask the question: does it fit with my unifier?

David also spent his life compartmentalizing what he did and then, depending on the person he was speaking to, would bring one of his roles to life. David wanted a personal unifier to help him understand what he really stood for, what was at his core. So he carried out the same exercise and ended up with these thoughts:

David

1 Writer:

- inspiring change;
- making the complex simple;
- telling stories.

2 Creative director:

- ideas that seduce;
- enabling creativity;
- leading teams.

3 Hypnotherapist:

- listening and understanding;
- eliciting answers;
- helping people find solutions.

The common denominator for David is change; when he looked back over his career he saw the successes were when he created change for individuals and companies. So David's unifier is a *change agent*. That description unites all he does and all he will do.

So now you can see that a unifier is more powerful than a job title. Because, let's face it, a job title can be pretty meaningless. After all, what exactly does the title 'Executive Vice-President' tell us anyway? Nilofer Merchant is a corporate director, speaker, and columnist in the *Harvard Business Review*. In a blog post entitled 'And who are you?' she wrote:

> **No amount of titles would make it clear my unique gifts in the world, or yours. Titles are simply false standards by which we come to define who we are. But, because they are so pervasive, we believe in them as a truth.**
>
> (Merchant, 2011)

Having that clarity for yourself as well as employers should not be underestimated, especially where your professional offering embraces so many elements. With a strong network of contacts it's not unusual to receive phone calls or e-mails saying 'I've got something you might be interested in' or 'Here's an opportunity for you' or 'Can I bounce something off you?' Often we'd rather say we're too busy, but we also know this is how lucrative opportunities start, so we need to listen. But having a unifier provides the criterion for whether this is a conversation worth having. A random call about something that does not fit the unifier means we can say 'Let me stop you there. That sounds interesting, but that's not what I do, so I can't help.' Your unifier is effectively a filter for whether you say 'yes' or 'no' to something. If it fits that unifier, go and have a coffee with that woman. If not, feel confident about saying 'no'.

So let's hear some examples of others who have found their unifiers. Sarah Beeny is best known to UK television viewers as the property expert presenter of *Property Ladder*. In addition to her TV show she founded a dating website, mysinglefriend.com, and another website where users can buy and sell property. To some it may look like her interests lack a common thread. Sarah explained to us that all her ventures are about making things 'simple and straightforward'. Her personal unifier means, however complex the problem, she finds the simple way to solve that problem and communicate the solution.

You might find your personal unifier in your own individual business style. Jose Castillo's work life includes writing about new media, speaking at conferences, and consulting with Fortune 500 companies and start-ups on the convergence of technology, marketing and ideas. With his wife he also runs a co-working space in his native Johnson City in Tennessee. We met Jose in London and discovered that his unifier is what he bills the 'spicy factor'. Through all his projects Jose strives to invest that 'extra spice' clients are looking for. Some of his spicy projects include leading panels in Silicon Valley, starting up a company focused on new media business, and launching a monthly 'Geek Dinner'. Jose landed on his unifier when a designer created his logo featuring a caricature with a chilli pepper light bulb. Jose realized that's what he does: injecting a little flavour, a little spice, into dull projects.

Your unifier is at the heart of your offering, and once you have identified it and communicated it to the outside world you can use it as the foundation to build upon. Phill Jupitus may do a number of things in 'showbiz', but being a stand-up comedian remains his unifier. The ability to 1) think quickly, 2) raise a laugh and 3) be topical has won him roles in West End musicals and regular slots on BBC radio panel shows. Phill told us that being a stand-up gives you a flexible skill set that you can apply beyond the microphone, as you can also probably act and present. These are natural by-products of being a good stand-up. Having those skills is why a TV show hired him and why he got a newspaper column. Over a coffee on a cold December morning before Christmas, Phill told us:

Stand-up is the frame that everything hangs off – it's the Christmas tree and everything else is just baubles.

So for Phill it's stand-up, for Sarah simplicity and for Jose adding spice. Your unifier will become a very powerful tool for internalizing what you do and enabling you to tell your story succinctly, sell your talents or decide whether to take that coffee meeting. So ditch the job title and find an authentic unifier!

Name: Sarah Graham

Location: London

Bio: Psychotherapist, counsellor, writer and editor

1   **So tell us your multidimensional talents, how you earn a living.** I'm currently working as a psychotherapist and counsellor with young people and adults, am supervising psychotherapy students and am a freelance writer and editor.

2   **When did you transition to go plural?** When I started training as a therapist 10 years ago, I left a full-time job in public relations and went freelance to pay the bills while I was training and working for free as a therapist. It felt like a leap of faith at the time but I was never short of work – even during the recession(s). I was always able to pick up a range of projects or short-/long-term contracts.

3   **What's your strategy for answering the 'What do you do?' dinner party/pub question?** Actually for a while after I qualified, unsure about what to do next and self-conscious about 'not knowing', my answer was a little self-denigrating. But now I'm in my groove and relaxed about not having a clear 'label' – in fact I'm quite proud of that! So I might give an overview of my work life or focus on a specific role, depending on who's asking the question. I don't label what I do, but focus more on the type of work I'm involved in.

4   **How do you sell your multidimensional talents?** So far I have generated work through word-of-mouth recommendation, but I plan to develop a more comprehensive marketing approach in the coming months and years.

5   What are the joys of a work life where you mash up different talents? Once I qualified I thought the portfolio approach might disappear as I forged my new career, but actually I love having a variety of work projects and being in charge of my own business: deciding who I work with, what I do, and when I do it. I enjoy working with different people from different strands of life, and I love not being in an office from nine to five, Monday to Friday. And I like that it allows me to keep my options open – I feel I have the freedom to follow a direction that excites me and am well placed to make the most of new opportunities that might present themselves in the future.

6   And what are your pain points in doing more than one thing? Having to be responsive to several 'bosses' and riding out the squeeze points when there are a number of deadlines all hitting at the same time. Sometimes the anxiety levels increase when there's no work on the horizon, but over the years I've learnt to trust that something always turns up (it always does).

HOW TO MAKE SURE
THAT YOU ARE GOING TO
GET THE MOST OUT OF
PLURAL LIVING BY WORKING
OUT WHAT MOTIVATES YOU.

05

What's driving you?

There are different reasons we find ourselves mashing up. Perhaps it's a desire to prove to yourself and those around you that you are capable of scratching more than one itch? Or perhaps you're just looking to earn more money? As Terence Watts explained in Chapter 2, our respective personality types have different attributes that make us suited (or not) to living the plural life. But, in order to ensure that you are getting the most out of mashing, you need to know what motivates you. And it all starts with asking yourself some important questions...

David Hieatt, entrepreneur and co-founder of the Do Lectures, told us:

> I started the Do Lectures, which I don't get paid by, but it helps me meet lots of amazing people, which is brilliant. It is good to do something for no return sometimes. It has given back to me many, many times.

People like David Hieatt are successful at doing more than one thing for one reason: they are driven. Without that drive, nothing will happen. The driving force that demands success and perseveres until you reach it is emotional. That driver may be 15 per cent rational, but it is 85 per cent emotional. So does your multiple work life get your heart racing? A racing heart means you will be emotionally driven, and that emotion is a powerful motivator. If the concept of a multidimensional work life doesn't turn you on, you won't make it a success.

Nothing kills the passion for life quite like doing something that is not you. It is not unusual for people to get pulled in one direction, say towards the money, and neglect to invest in the passion too. What happens next is they start to feel something is missing. But they think about it and then say, 'Well, I'm earning good money so what can this problem be?' Next they feel dissatisfied with work, they start looking around for something new and consider how much greener the grass must be on the other side, and so they crave change. But once they make that change they feel dissatisfied again, having become reminded of why they made their initial change. This confusion born from not finding balance is a common story. The money on its own will not do. The love on its own will not do. You must find the balance in what is driving you and be honest about that.

When we spoke to Terence Watts he was adamant that before you embark on your journey you *must* be totally honest with yourself about *why* you are doing it. More money? Admiration from others? Passion? These are all the secret drivers that live within us, guiding our actions towards our goals both consciously and subconsciously. So whatever the true reason you must be totally accepting of that and not feel compelled to say something else when asked. If you want more money, good, say that. You can see how internal conflict can come about if you are feeling one thing inside and saying another. Your real reasons are your own real reasons, and you can celebrate those reasons; otherwise, as Terence Watts put it, 'hidden barriers will appear'. By being true to yourself you will move much faster towards what it is you desire and you will find happiness with it too.

Here are some examples of what might be driving you:

→ **Talent:** Some people have more than one talent or skill and rather than be restricted to delivering just one of them they will get fulfilment from doing more than one thing.

→ **Opportunity:** Many people have spotted a niche in the market, an opportunity they can explore as a side project, launching a new business or exploring an idea.

→ **Survival:** In a tough job market where competition is fierce, survival is about having the right skills at the right time. Being plural can give you the edge.

→ **Philanthropy:** You might have a yearning desire to help people or volunteer for a charity.

→ **Standing out:** Not everyone wants to appear like everyone else – a plural work life gives you the licence to be different.

→ **Money:** You may have the chance to transform an idea into cash. Adding a new string to your bow means you have another potential revenue stream.

→ **Passion:** Many people are so passionate about wine, or coffee, or cycling that it becomes their side project. They're driven by spending time engrossed in something they love.

→ **Collaboration:** This is about the buzz that comes from collaborating with others, being part of something bigger than yourself.

→ **Control:** You may want to be in control of your own destiny: the notion that you can create the life you want to lead.

So which one is driving you? The above is not an exhaustive list – there are many others. Also remember: it doesn't have to be just one. In fact, like us, you'll have different drivers for different elements. But knowing what drives you means you can rationalize what you're doing and why. And don't forget: emotion is a powerful driver in itself. So don't be shy of getting emotional about what you're doing and why you're doing it and who you're doing it for.

Our own drivers are multiple. Ian gets driven from creating something out of nothing, having some interesting stories to tell; David gets driven by curiosity and the chance to produce positive change by applying creative thinking, psychology and innovation.

Comedian Phill Jupitus explained to us that he has multiple drivers that motivate him. So when he is offered a new role he checks the offer against three questions: 1) Is it interesting? 2) If it's a play or a musical is it good? 3) Do the people seem interesting to work with?

Multidimensional writer Mark Hillary summed up the idea of working only with interesting people slightly differently. He said:

❝ The joy is in having a lot of control in how to spend my time. I can be flexible in my working hours, and with a lot of different activities if someone annoys me then I won't work with them again.

So you need to recognize what your drivers are. When answering, tell the truth, the whole truth and nothing but the truth. We sometimes tend to be quite concerned about how others see us. We care about what they may think and how they will react to what we say. So we choose our words carefully and describe things as others will want to hear them rather than as we believe them to be. Forget all that, dig deep and make sure you're honest about what really drives you, what will really get you out of bed in the morning, what will really get you productive and successful.

Name: Steve Sampson

Location: Hertfordshire, England

Bio: Zookeeper, entrepreneur

1   **So tell us your multidimensional talents, how you earn a living.** I am very lucky, as I love what I do. I live in the middle of Paradise Wildlife Park with white lions in my front garden. I wake up to the sound of lemurs, gibbons and tigers roaring. Paradise Wildlife Park is also where I am based and from where I get paid. We have owned Paradise for 27 years, and it was widely regarded as the worst zoo in Britain when we bought it in 1984. We are very proud of the fact that we are now one of the leading private zoos in Europe. I also run three other businesses. These are Sussed, a project management, training and sales promotion company, My Rewards Company, which operates white label corporate rewards programmes, and Ginicam, which is an online trading platform. I have owned many businesses over the years, including a bus advertising company, wholesale meat company, balloon company and a radio station, which was a financial disaster!

2   **When did you transition to go plural?** We have always been involved in other business. This stemmed from my dad, Peter, who started the family business and a number of other successful businesses. I am very much the son of my father and a child at heart that loves new projects. There is a real challenge to getting a business started, and my skill sets seem to suit this environment. It is about vision and drive and inspiring the people around you by creating a fertile environment where ideas can grow and mature. I am very much broad brush and not great on detail. I have however learnt to

ensure I have a good team around me to dot the i's and cross the t's.

3   **What's your strategy for answering the 'What do you do?' dinner party/pub question?** There is no better invitation than asking someone if they would like to come and feed a tiger. We have arguably the best collection of big cats across our two sites, Paradise Wildlife Park in Hertfordshire and the Big Cat Sanctuary in Kent. It gets very complicated and messy if I try to explain all of the projects I am involved with. The animals are by far the most sexy and the easiest way to hook people in. We also do an incredible amount of conservation work around the globe, which people are genuinely interested in, so we usually make popular guests.

4   **How do you sell your multidimensional talents?** It is not a case of selling your multidimensional talents but being able to appreciate your skill set, so you can concentrate on what you are good at and bring in other people to cover your shortfalls. It has taken me 49 years to really appreciate this and I could have saved myself a lot of time, money and heartache if I had sussed this out earlier in my working life. I now try to surround myself with talented people and ensure they have the confidence and authority to flourish through delegation. I see myself as a facilitator assisting other people around achieving their goals.

5   **What are the joys of a work life where you mash up different talents?** Every day is different. This is the real joy of my work life. I don't actually see it as work though, as I enjoy it so much. I am also in a fortunate position where I can choose what I do and who I work with. I have complete freedom to decide what I do and

more importantly do not do! This can bring pressure and sometimes creates situations where you tend to go it alone rather than delegating to the people around you. There are of course days when things go completely wrong, but as a very good friend once said to me you need to be like a 'weeble-wobble', which was a kids' toy that if you knocked it down it bounced straight back up. It is rare to get two bad days back to back, so you know tomorrow will be better with fresh challenges.

6   **And what are your pain points in doing more than one thing?** It is the continual plate spinning that sometimes is a grind. I am conscious of the fact that none of the businesses are getting my undivided attention and therefore opportunities are missed and time is wasted. People around me get frustrated, as they are sometimes waiting for me to react or answer queries they have raised. We work exceptionally long hours, which does help get things done, and we work hard to create a positive environment. I, like most people who own their business, know that I do not spend enough time with my family. We do however have a great life and experience many amazing things. You cannot beat having young lions and tigers living in your house!

BY THINKING PLURAL
YOU CAN OPEN YOUR HEART
AND MIND TO A NEW WORLD
OF POSSIBILITIES.

06

Adopting a portable mindset

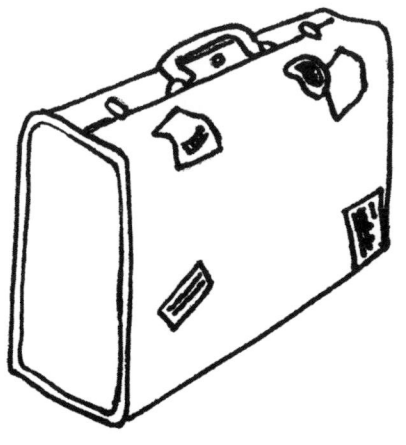

Mashing is a portable mindset that you can take and apply to every business situation. Instead of a single focus that risks closing down options, by thinking plural you can open your heart and mind to a new world of possibilities. You can consider how and where plural thinking will add value . This mindset will allow you to go on a journey of discovery that will ensure your work life and professional interests are as varied and as eclectic as your iTunes library.

A flexible mindset is not just necessary for juggling multiple projects; you also need flexibility in your working practices, ie where and how you work. Just as sometimes you'll work better with a notepad and pen than a laptop, other times the kitchen table may be a more productive place to work than a desk in the office.

If you do more than one thing the chances are you'll need more than one place to do it from. Why? Because we are heavily influenced by context – our surroundings influence our thinking and our behaviour. So experience has taught us that doing everything from your Starbucks or everything from your desk is possibly not the best solution. It's rarely a case of one size fits all. Our editor Liz works some days from her publishing office in Islington, another day from home or the coffee shop, alongside having meetings in a hotel lobby or a restaurant. Like the best mashers Liz knows where she works best and what she needs to throw at each bit of her life.

It's a similar story with Lynda Gratton, the London Business School academic, writer and management consultant who heads her own research company, the Hot Spots Movement. Although Lynda has an office in London's Somerset House, this is just a focal point for her research company and a space where she can share ideas and collaborate with other tenants in the building. She also works from home in London's Primrose Hill, from her weekend home in Sitges and at an office at London Business School. As Aparna Piramal Raje said in a profile of Lynda Gratton, 'her multiple workplaces reflect her many avatars' (Raje, 2011). Lynda acknowledges that she has a very organized approach to her multidimensional work life, as she needs to juggle writing books with conducting a workshop for a client, speaking and researching.

Unsurprisingly both of us are also nomadic in our work lives – that mirrors the variety of the roles we execute. So we spend a lot of our lives in coffee shops, members' clubs, co-working spaces and trains. We save the desk, the normal place of work for many, for our admin.

Some mashers take this further by becoming 'location-independent'. That term is given to the growing tribe of people who are proving that they can truly be anywhere on Planet Earth to do their work. Mark Hillary, the blogger, writer and technology expert, recently moved to Brazil; he wanted to prove that he could work from anywhere without it affecting his work. When he left the UK, Mark was working for clients in France, Ukraine, the Czech Republic and India in addition to the UK. Now he is in Brazil he has managed to retain almost all those earlier clients alongside new work coming from within Brazil – so the move has expanded his work possibilities. To maintain the UK relationships he just makes sure he visits the country a few times a year, but like many of us Mark of course uses the internet to deliver everything he does. He used to have a contract with a company in Reading (England) but he never once visited their offices, instead meeting them at conferences in the UK and overseas. His value was based on deliverables and results, not time spent at a desk. Mark says:

❝ Once you go into a multidimensional working environment where clients are all over the place and expect different things at different times, the idea of a nine-to-five life is meaningless. You could work more hours, or less, but the bottom line is that you only get paid if you deliver what the client wants.

If your client or employer is seeking results and that is what you are going to be measured by then they will rarely care where you do it from and how you do it. They will be interested in the outputs, so you are free to find the space and time that delivers the maximum output. And that applies not just to working life but also to non-work time. Stephanie Booth takes a two-month break to India for January and February, but it's not just a holiday – it's an integral part of her mindset that ultimately delivers value for clients. As her auto-response says: 'Sorry for any inconvenience... but being able to take time off is what allows me to remain creative and productive for my clients.'

Not only that but, to help her, Steph's auto-response also told us she would not be looking at any e-mails until March. That's a great tactic for avoiding dealing with two months' worth of e-mail on her return.

Kevin Roberts, CEO of Saatchi & Saatchi, told us 'Inspiration out is a big result of inspiration in', so you need to take inspiration from what's outside in the real world, not from e-mails and search engines.

Get inspired, or re-inspired if you like; go back to that place where you felt energized and ready to change the world. That ability to stay inspired, productive and motivated is part of your portable mindset.

If you are stuck where to seek inspiration, perhaps go to a museum or art gallery with fresh eyes, or visit a market and see how the stallholders set out their wares. See what it is you like and look with fresh eyes. Take all these gut instincts to help inspire you. Start a scrapbook and add to it anything and everything you find inspiring. Ian and David carry a Moleskine notebook with them everywhere to capture those moments of inspiration as they happen. It could be a quote, an article, a photograph, something torn out of a newspaper or a promotional flyer. It might open up some interesting directions that you would have never otherwise stumbled upon that end up delivering huge commercial value to you and your project.

If you are making the leap to mash-up then some of these ideas may sound radical. Maybe you don't want to go on sabbatical to Goa or work out of coffee shops. That's cool with us. Just do whatever works for you. Maybe you would prefer a single workspace, in which case that is what you must do. If you prefer to move between spaces as you work on different projects then feel free to do that too. Whatever stimulates productivity is key here. You will be delivering multiple skills to multiple clients, so find your rhythm, find your groove.

Name: Sejal Parekh

Location: London

Twitter: @holasejal

Twitter Bio: "Comms & Digital lover. Director@triflecreative. Former head of comms @wearewhatif"

1   **So tell us your multidimensional talents, how you earn a living.** Director of triflecreative* workspace design company. My role involves day-to-day running of the business, small company growth strategy through to insight-led designing, client management, pitching, running a project, managing suppliers, sourcing, buying, managing people. We try to stay close to the actual work and clients, as that's very important to us.

Strategic communications and innovation 'consultant'. Working with a range of companies on business challenges, marketing and communications strategies, PR both traditional and non-traditional, and content generation and curation.

It all comes down to helping people (companies) better communicate, whether it be how they work together, shouting about stuff they've done or communicating new products or services to consumers.

2   **When did you transition to go plural?** It wasn't a conscious decision actually; necessity kind of brought it about. Then I started enjoying it and realizing how having different facets, different clients, different approaches was super-interesting and provided challenges and lots of learning.

3 **What's your strategy for answering the 'What do you do?' dinner party/pub question?** I haven't got this nailed yet. Wonder if I ever will? It very much depends on the audience. It usually starts with 'Well, I do a couple of different things...' People who just want to hear a job title or company name aren't going to be interested in my story (and probably me about theirs!). I believe that most people are unlikely to do the same thing every day, day in day out. Their jobs are multifaceted and involved; they have to put on different hats and use different skills to their job and do it well. That's a given; no one questions that, but if you don't fit a conventional box it either unnerves or excites people. I want to be with the excited people.

4 **How do you sell your multidimensional talents?** It depends on who I'm 'selling' it to; there are still so many people who cannot accept you can be great (or in their minds an expert) if you don't fit a pigeonhole. I just try to get to know them and them me. I try to bring to life my experience or expertise through examples, stories that will resonate with them. Once they really get to know me they realize that having these different facets is often what makes me able to do things differently and creatively.

5 **What are the joys of a work life where you mash up different talents?** Learning from different worlds, continually having different perspectives on things and clients. I learn so much about how companies are run, their cultures, how people interact, and that feeds both sides of my work. Sometimes they overlap and that is the optimum for me! As tenuous as it might sound on paper they are interlinked. For me it's all about how people can better communicate (whether it be to each other or to clients and consumers). Also working this way allows me to satisfy or at least explore both the strategic and creative drive in me.

6   **And what are your pain points in doing more than one thing?** Feeling thinly stretched or that you're not excelling at any one thing. Both aspects of what I do go in peaks and troughs, which generally are at different times, but you can't control that, so when they both peak or both trough it is tough. The above points outweigh these feelings and issues though!

KNOWING HOW YOUR MULTIPLE SKILLS CAN WORK BETTER TOGETHER TO CREATE MULTI-SKILL HARMONY.

07

How to harmonize your different skills

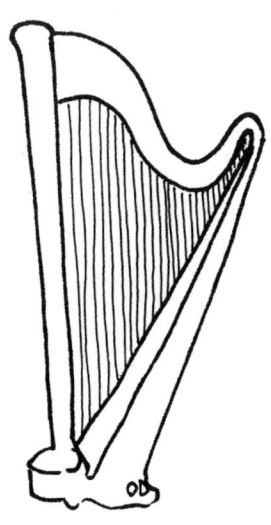

Knowing how your multiple skills can work better together and create more value is key to improving your mash-up life. As with a DJ on the turntables or a chef in the kitchen, it is the mixing together of seemingly disparate ingredients that produces the interesting results. Who would have thought that a rap-meets-country remix could create a compelling sound? Who would have imagined that bacon mixed with ice cream could be so tasty? These creations are seldom the accidental fusion of opposites. They are much more likely a calculation based on a criterion, in the case of music, key and tempo; in the case of food, tastes, colours and textures. So what can we learn from the dance floor and the kitchen when it comes to adding a new ingredient to your skill set and, more importantly, how do you find the common denominator that creates multi-skill harmony?

The job of the DJ is to give the crowd rhythm and pace that compel them to dance. The experienced DJ will do this by mixing and blending music that is familiar to the audience as an individual song but will be a new experience for the audience as a soundscape. On the surface, for the audience, it is easy to understand – the music is uninterrupted and familiar. But behind the scenes something else is going on in the mind of the DJ, who is ensuring that the next track is in key with the previous one, has a similar energy, complements the tempo and moves the set forward. The DJ can switch between genres, use effects, speed up and slow down a song to a degree, but ultimately the final mix must be harmonious. The same can be said for the chef: all the individual ingredients may be from different countries, be different colours and taste entirely unique, but the chef will be judged by the harmonious coming together of the flavours. We can learn a lot from chefs and DJs as we contemplate our careers. Will our own story be harmonious? So we must be mindful as we add new strings to our bows that these are harmonious with what we already have. Mashing is not jumping from one disparate career to the next; it's marrying opportunities that serve to add value to your true DNA. The multidimensional Gary Vaynerchuk has interests that encompass marketing, wine, business, social media and sports. Gary told us, 'I want my brand to be my DNA', and you should do the same.

When introducing the iPad 2 in 2011, Steve Jobs explained:

▟▟ It is in Apple's DNA that technology alone is not enough – it's technology married with liberal arts, married with the humanities, that yields us the results that make our hearts sing.

Jobs' own experience was about applying what he'd learnt in calligraphy school to designing the first Macintosh computer 10 years later. That understanding and appreciation of typefaces became a key differentiator of Apple products, as Jobs reveals in his biography:

▟▟ It was the first computer with beautiful typography. If I had never dropped in on that single course in college, the Mac would never have had multiple typefaces or proportionally spaced fonts.

(Isaacson, 2011)

When multiple skills begin to work together they will increase the output potential. Having become well known as the co-founder of LastMinute.com, Martha Lane Fox now has a portfolio that includes: founder of a karaoke bar Lucky Voice, a role as the UK government's Digital Inclusion Champion, together with charity interests and non-executive director roles at companies including Channel 4 and M&S:

❝ It hadn't been my plan to end up with this portfolio of interests quite so young. By being across many different things you bring something a bit more interesting to each thing you're doing. I certainly think I do a better job at Lucky Voice having been aware of what's happening at M&S for example.

How can you create harmony like this? What is the blend of ingredients that you need in your kitchen?

Meet Andy. He is 26 and works as a freelance fashion photographer. He has had the worst year on record and fears that he will have to switch career if something doesn't change. He has very good 'soft' skills: he enjoys being around people, conversation and listening. His 'hard' skills are pure photography based: cameras and associated editing. He arranges a meeting with his main contacts to ask what has changed in the industry that will explain the drop in work. The feedback he gets is that a single picture from Andy normally costs £1,000 – now they need to see more content for the same money. His clients suggest that if he could provide more content with the photos he shoots he would most likely get more work.

Armed with this information Andy reflects on his soft and hard skills: so he's good with people, and also understands cameras and editing. Then he has an idea. He calls a model who he has photographed many times before and asks if she will come to his studio for an unpaid test shoot. Andy goes through his normal procedure with her, all the time engaging his subject in conversation. His camera is capable of filming high definition video, so at the end of taking stills he films a conversation with the model where she explains what goes on behind the scenes in a model's life. The film, when edited, is a compelling insight into the life of a model. He shows the film to his clients and it fits their needs: Andy is now the photographer who also delivers beautifully composed and compelling video content. By harmonizing his hard and soft skills, Andy was able to grow his talents and his business.

The trick to creating harmony is to look for small changes that will make a big difference. Andy needed to recognize his people skills and use those to create a new revenue stream. When you set out to find your harmony don't be fooled into thinking it has to be an obvious career progression. It should reflect the needs of both your industry and your passions. But what if your needs are less pressing and you are driven by a more personal need to harmonize your many talents?

Frances Booth has two different skills: writer and photographer. We came across her when David saw her business cards on display in a co-working space in East London. She had two different cards, side by side: one selling her skills as a writer; a completely different one for her skills as a photographer. She has two business identities and websites to match: 'Here are some words' (herearesomewords.com) and 'Here are some pictures' (herearesomepictures.com).

Frances told us she earns a living mainly from the writing, editing and training side of her business. One day she will be training a roomful of people in how to write for the web; the next, she'll be rewriting a 1,000-word blog for an entrepreneur. This is the words. Then there's the pictures. She'd been training and shooting to build up her skills for around two years before she launched her photography site, but had been a keen photographer for many years. This was a natural extension, to mix up words and pictures. Going with the pictures was a no-brainer, as she didn't put too much financial pressure on it. She knew she could use words to make a living while slowly building up pictures: she was in harmony.

That sense of harmony is just as important in reconciling the different drivers for what you're doing, balancing for example things you do for love with things you do for money. We're fans of Hugh MacLeod since we saw him speak at the South by Southwest (SXSW) festival in 2009. In his book *Ignore Everybody: And 39 Other Keys to Creativity*, he explains what he calls his 'Sex and Cash Theory':

The creative person basically has two kinds of jobs: one is the sexy creative kind. Second is the kind that pays the bills. Sometimes the task at hand covers both bases, but not often. This tense duality will also play center stage. It will never be transcended.

(MacLeod, 2009)

But it's important to remember there's no grand strategy for achieving harmony. Sometimes it's about what feels right. Let's look at the multidimensional Baratunde Thurston. Baratunde is well known as the Digital Editor of the satirical news site *The Onion*; he's also a regular at the SXSW Interactive 'geek fest' in Texas. He describes himself as 'a politically active, technology-loving comedian from the future'. He's a stand-up comic and is author of the new book *How to Be Black*. He told *Fast Company* magazine (February 2012):

I was a computer programmer in high school, but I discovered I wasn't very good at it – it was too tedious. I was a philosophy major. I did management consulting right out of college. But then I started doing comedy, and I love it. People say to me all the time, 'What are you? You need to focus.' Maybe so. But for now, this smorgasbord of activities is working.

(Safian, 2012)

Like taste, harmony can be subjective. One person's idea of perfect harmony may not be a tasty dish for someone else. Whether you create harmony through a strategy like Andy or go with what feels right like Baratunde, the end result is the same – creating that blend of ingredients that delivers fulfilment and commercial opportunities and gives you an edge.

Name: Jose Castillo

Location: Johnson City, Tennessee

Twitter: @thinkjose

Twitter Bio: "Spicy things! Like content-editor for online video @StreamingMedia & being Entertainment Captain for @BMSUpdates"

1   **So tell us your multidimensional talents, how you earn a living.** When my mother-in-law asks what I do for a living, I usually tell her I work for the CIA. It's easier than trying to explain all the things I am involved with. But most of my exploits fall into speaking, writing and consulting. On the speaking side I have several MC jobs and I also speak at conferences and workshops around the world. I have been the voice and face for seven years at Bristol Motor Speedway. As 'entertainment captain' my job is to interview fans, drivers and celebrities on the jumbotron. I have led two Guinness World Records, ridden around the world's fastest half-mile in a NASCAR stock car and had more exciting interactions with some of the best fans in the world. I also MC WillThisFloat?, a business idea pitch game show, and I love helping entrepreneurs launch their own businesses. I write for two magazines, *Streaming Media* and *EContent*, and do occasional freelance work. I also own and operate several start-ups, including our region's first co-working space called SparkPlaza.com. It's a lot but I love it!

2   **When did you transition to go plural?** I have always done multiple things at once. I like to start spicy things, and the drive to constantly find new things keeps me on the go. As a kid I worked for my dad's advertising agency, sold T-shirts at my high school and worked at

the local chicken restaurant. It's never been easy for me to focus on one thing, so I have tried to work that into a positive. I started the thinkjose.com blog while I was working as a senior account executive for an interactive agency. It's always good to have multiple outlets for work.

3   What's your strategy for answering the 'What do you do?' dinner party/pub question? I tell people I start spicy things and slide them a sticker with my website on it. (Stickers are more fun than business cards.) Sometimes it's hard for people when they can't label you right off, but I like being able to not be defined. It's hard enough to get to know someone even if they have a clear job title. Besides, I love meeting new people, not new job titles.

4   How do you sell your multidimensional talents? Good old-fashioned word of mouth! And, yes, the social media scene has made that a lot easier and harder. Now everyone can be a guru of this or a wizard of that, but the proof is in your work. When you do something spicy and dramatically different, people will talk about it. That drives sales.

5   What are the joys of a work life where you mash up different talents? Every day is the day when something fresh, new and exciting will jump out at you. I also love being able to cross-pollinate ideas. Being able to take something you learn from MCing and apply it to writing is very cool. There is never a lack of new ideas out there, and being in multiple industries gives you a much broader view on overall trends and patterns.

6 **And what are your pain points in doing more than one thing?** The pain points for a mash-up work life are the same as the joys. Everything is new every day and you have to be agile and willing to work harder. Keeping up with one industry in this overloaded information age is tough; try keeping up with six! It's impossible to clone yourself, so you must find people and resources that will be just as nimble and excited as yourself. Working for one organization can give the false sense of security, regular pay cheque, benefits, etc, but working across multiple genres can be up and down in the revenue department. Be prepared for more lean times, but also the rewards are so much greater. I can't imagine living a life that isn't mashed up. Imagine eating the same meal every day for the rest of your life. Yes, you would get the nutrition you needed to sustain life, but with no variety, flavour or spice. Is that really a life worth living?

HOW TO GET STIMULATION
AND SATISFACTION BY
GETTING CLOSE TO THE
WORK LIFE THAT REFLECTS
THE REAL YOU.

The joy of mash

You may have a number of different drivers for creating a plural work life. But one net result for doing more than one thing is that, whatever the challenges, you'll love the variety. We do! You'll get stimulation and satisfaction from getting as close as you can to your work life reflecting the real you, embracing your interests and passions. And that means you can have some F-U-N.

Recently we met a zookeeper called Steve Sampson. Steve isn't your usual zookeeper; mind you, we haven't met any others, but we guess he isn't typical. Whilst our kids took a look at the penguins, one Saturday morning over a coffee in his office Steve showed us his latest project, a web-based idea that has nothing to do with big cats. He also outlined a consumer rewards business he'd just launched and a consultancy project he's involved with. Ian asked Steve what was driving all this stuff, this desire to do so many different things. Steve's answer was simple:

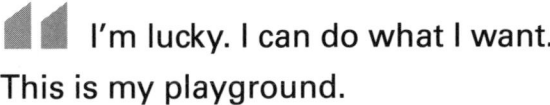 **I'm lucky. I can do what I want. This is my playground.**

You might not expect to meet such an enterprising zookeeper, mashing up technology and an animal park, but it's just a reflection of who he is and what he wants to do. Steve's primary objective is having fun.

When you get it right, mashing it up is like throwing paint around in your playroom. Popular media may be bashing you over the head with the impending disasters you face, but you should feel no guilt in being happy. You should not hide it if you enjoy what you do. Happiness is a state of mind, and just because the press reports only the negative you are under no obligation to echo that sentiment. True happiness comes from a feeling of internal satisfaction. It is not derived from regret.

Our parents' generation was about that career ladder, climbing the rungs from bank clerk to prestigious director status with all the perks to match, and then retirement with a nice pension. Those days are gone. Vanished. Say goodbye. When you live the mashed-up life, you won't have those traditional indicators of career success: job titles, promotions, successive climbs of rungs on the job ladder. You'll need to find other benchmarks for success: the fact that you are passionate about getting out of bed in the morning, the fact that you have some interesting stories to share. So forget those old indicators of success, and embrace the joys of what this work life gives you. We don't know about you, but we'd rather have some interesting stories to share with our grandkids, sitting around the fire, than impress them with a bunch of job titles and perks we once had.

Take David's story. David trained as a journalist, not because he had aspirations of working for a national newspaper, but because he loved finding things out and telling the story. So he loves to mash because it gives him the licence to be curious and then to pursue that curiosity through to its end. The result may be learning a new skill or helping a company answer a business problem, or equally it may manifest itself as launching a business of his own. He is also an ideas man, so having fresh ideas and being able to investigate them gives him great pleasure and is often what pays the bills. David knows when he wakes in the morning that he has several projects, all that interest him, all that need thinking about, and he is free to find the right place, mindset and style to deliver them. No nine-to-five that demands him getting out of bed whilst he is in the middle of sketching out a solution, no defined structure that limits imagination, no compromising on making the process fun. Spontaneity is now a part of David's working week. If he gets stuck he may join the family for a trip to the zoo: no permission required, he can just do it. That trip, that freeing his mind for a few hours, will in most cases pay dividends in more ways than one. So David gets the satisfaction of a day out with the family as well as doing some work. His clients don't really care how, where or what tools he uses to solve their problem, they just want it solved. The satisfaction of not having to do that at a prescribed location in front of a work computer is something that David does not take for granted. He knows that as long as he can mash all the good stuff into the day then he has many reasons to smile.

The joy of mash for Ian is about being able to dip in and out of projects, shifting gears from one thing to another. Often he does that gear shifting in real time, so he may simultaneously have a number of documents open, brainstorming ideas, writing content, allowing a task he's doing in one area to bring value to a completely different one. Where some people neatly segment their week with separate roles on different days, Ian likes to mash it all together. Ian's learnt to enjoy that real-time mashing. But there's another benefit: freedom. Having 'hacked' or created a perfect job full of different elements, Ian is liberated to do things with no other agenda than that they would be cool to do. For example, Ian was always interested by the multidimensional life of the musician and entrepreneur Dave Stewart. So Ian decided to meet him and have a film-maker friend make a video of their chat. There was no great plan or agenda for this assignment; there was no 'ROI' other than 'That will be fun.' Since Ian works for himself and is accountable only to himself, he didn't have to clear it with anyone. So one Sunday he went to the Soho Hotel to meet Dave, making a video of his encounter. Of course the interesting thing is, once he'd made the film, he got his return on investment: getting paid to write an article on Dave for a website. But then something else happened. As a result of their meeting Ian connected with Dave on LinkedIn and then spotted a new connection: Dave's book editor Liz. Ian followed Liz on Twitter; she followed Ian back, and that led her to check out our work and offer us a book deal. Who could have predicted that? No one. But the motivator for doing it was to have fun. OK, so Ian may not have a job title and a company car and a career ladder, but it's a whole load of fun being master of your own destiny.

Stephanie Booth lives a multidimensional life in Switzerland and takes two months off every year to travel to India. As well as the extended break she gets joy from her 'patchwork of things' that takes in blogging, speaking, editing, training and acting as consultant. She thrives on that variety:

> I love that I can be doing strategic consulting for a tech start-up one day and giving a talk to schoolkid parents the next.

We hear this story a lot, how people have crafted these work lives that deliver happiness. We spoke to comedian Phill Jupitus, who told us he loves the opportunities his mashed-up life has given him. From interviewing his idol, the cartoonist Garry Trudeau, for a documentary on comic strips for BBC Radio 4 to appearing in the West End musical *Hairspray*, it all feels surreal:

❝ If you'd come up to me as a kid and picked six of the jobs I do and said you will be a breakfast DJ, you'll do a football column for *The Times* and you'll play a woman in a West End musical...!

Phill describes it as his 'Jim'll Fix It' life where he gets to do the dream job. He explained that, whilst he loves the stability of appearing on a regular TV show, he would get bored if that was all he did. The TV show has given him the commercial stability to build a multidimensional career around.

We won't pretend that living the mashed-up life will put a smile on your face 24/7. After all, doing more stuff is admittedly tougher than doing just one thing. But if you can succeed in carving out a plural work life that reflects your talents and desires then the chances are you're going to be more passionate about what you're doing. And whether it's interviewing your idols, writing a book or deciding to make time to learn circus skills – there definitely is joy in the mash.

Name: Paul Benney

Location: London

Twitter: @paulbenney

Twitter Bio: "I work at Brille (The Knife, Random Impulse), Dummy, Bugged Out and Decked Out. Jockey Slut RIP"

1   **So tell us your multidimensional talents, how you earn a living.** I part-own a number of companies in the music industry including a record company, publishing company, management company, events company and a DJ/live agency. I also part-own a music magazine style website. I earn my living mainly from my role as joint managing director of the record company, with the balance coming from dividends and profit shares from the other companies.

2   **When did you transition to go plural?** My first business when I left university was self-publishing a dance music magazine, and the events company was a natural progression from that (because of the opportunity to promote our own events in the magazine). This was the early nineties, so the internet didn't exist for most people, and events were almost solely publicized by press advertising, posters and flyers. For similar reasons a record label seemed a natural progression – we found records we wanted to sign at the club nights we promoted and via the magazine we published. We were then able to promote the releases in the magazine and book the artists who made them to play at the club nights. The knowledge and contacts gained from these businesses led to the management business and the DJ/live agency. We were booking so many artists from other agencies that we thought 'Wouldn't it be great if we could book

artists to play our events from our own agency?' So we set one up, recruited the DJs that played the club, and it has been successful for over 10 years now. The music publishing company and the music magazine style website follow the same thinking – they are businesses that complement the other companies I am involved in and are also able to exploit opportunities that the other businesses provide.

3   **What's your strategy for answering the 'What do you do?' dinner party/pub question?** I say I work in the music industry. If asked to be more specific I say I run an independent record label, as that is what I spend the majority of my time working on.

4   **How do you sell your multidimensional talents?** When signing artists to the label or the management company my involvement in the other businesses can be useful. Experience is the most valuable 'talent' in the music industry.

5   **What are the joys of a work life where you mash up different talents?** Approaching issues with different hats on can help keep things feeling fresh.

6   **And what are your pain points in doing more than one thing?** I sometimes worry that I may be in danger of spreading myself too thin. Also the admin associated with running one company can be tedious and time-consuming, but if you have a number of companies then the amount of admin involved is greatly increased. I have to be careful to make sure that I still have time left to actually work on developing the businesses.

HOW TO COMMUNICATE
YOUR TALENTS CLEARLY
SO THAT PEOPLE CAN
UNDERSTAND WHAT YOU DO.

Crafting your mashed-up story

To get the full benefit of having multiple skills you'll need to be able to communicate your talents clearly so that people can understand – and recall – what you do. Your story is what people will remember you by and is what they will share with others to explain who you are. Think of your story as your road to fame. Your great story will get passed around and, one conversation at a time, you will become famous. So don't be a secret masher: have a story and get good at telling it.

Having a disparate mix of skills can sound complicated to others. And that's where your story is a powerful tool in making the complicated simple. For example, you meet a woman who tells you she's a garden designer, dog walker and website builder. Without understanding the context of that bunch of work stuff, how do you follow on from that introduction? However, if the same person had said 'I love design and I love animals. Online I design beautiful websites, offline I design beautiful gardens and in between I walk beautiful dogs . I love it', you would totally get it. This person has a passion for design, in both the analogue world and the digital world, and also loves animals. When you hear a story you get it. But it's not always that way.

We were sitting in an Oxford coffee shop recently. A bloke having a meeting one table away recognized a woman at another. It was clear by the initial recognition that they had not seen each other for a long time. 'What are you up to?' she asked. 'I run a little PR company from home', he said, before adding that inevitable postscript, 'amongst other things.' And he left it at that. She exited the coffee shop thinking her old friend was only in PR (or 'little PR' as he described it). He hadn't been clear in communicating the breadth of his ventures; he hadn't honed his story. So it got left at that: a little PR company. What are his other buyable skills? Who knows, but for the purpose of explaining how important it is that you have your story we will say that he also ran an events company and managed party entertainers. So we can see how by not explaining his 'amongst other things' properly he failed to maximize the random encounter. He became, by default, a secret masher destined to be forgotten by everyone who asks him what he does and receives the 'little PR company amongst other things' reply.

Now if that chance encounter woman requires an events company he will not get the call. If her next office party requires an entertainer he will not get the call. With every person she meets or speaks to about needing an entertainer or looking for help with an event, that bloke will not come to mind, so he will not get the call. And if someone asks the woman for a little PR company? He probably still won't get the call, because he failed to give her a story, just a simplified definition of a job title. What kind of sector does he deliver PR for? Does he cover online PR? Offline PR? Both? Does he deliver social media? He is not memorable for one simple reason: he failed to draw any kind of picture in the mind of the listener, and he didn't offer her a business card. That is why we need to be brilliant at telling our story.

So what makes a story? A story requires a beginning that sets the scene for what is to follow. There is then a middle section, which will benefit from including a little tension. Then you can finish with an ending that makes sense when heard in the context of the beginning and middle. In the example of the PR bloke in the coffee shop, he could have said: 'Let me tell you how my life changed. I was head of PR and events at X corporation. Like many people I woke up one morning and thought "What the hell am I doing with my life?" So that day I walked into my boss's office and said "Here's my notice." I turned around and marched out. I never looked back. Now I run my own PR and events company and, to keep me laughing, I manage entertainers too. It's the best thing I ever did. Here's my card. Take it; don't try telling me you never need to book a balloon sculptor; everyone needs a laugh.' You can see how that story is much more powerful and memorable than 'I run a little PR company... amongst other things.' If people remember your story they will pass it on to others.

Whether you are leaving the comfort of your job or adding a new skill to your toolbox you will need to update your story, your new story that will work for a random meeting in the coffee shop and can be summed up for online use, a new story that will act as your advert. The better your advert the more of an advantage you will have against your competition. Dave Trott is a legendary adman and the brains behind many classic TV commercials. He has created adverts that made products famous, and the message had to be delivered in 30 seconds. He couldn't say 'Oh, this advert will need to be two minutes long, as I have lots to say.' He had to deliver everything in a 30-second slot, and it had to work hard to make products and brands famous. His creations are so well known that many years later people still recall his adverts for Pepsi and Toshiba with a nostalgic smile. So what's his formula?

During a recent seminar Dave broke advertising down into three key elements. The first is **impact**. The very first thing you need to do is get the attention of the person you want to speak to. The second is **communication**. You must communicate clearly what it is you want people to know. The third is

persuasion. You will need to persuade people to use your service over the competition's offering.

That is very easy to understand (Dave Trott is not a man to complicate things unnecessarily), but all too often it is not put into practice. Some adverts fail to have impact, as do some people fail to have impact ('Who is she again?'). Some adverts fail to communicate clearly the benefit of what they offer, as do some people fail to communicate the benefit they offer ('What does she do again?'). Some adverts fail to persuade you to take action, just as some people fail to persuade you to take action ('Sorry, I haven't got her e-mail address; she didn't give me her business card').

So let's return to the Bristol coffee shop. 'I run a little PR company amongst other things.' Impact: none. Communication: none. Persuasion: none. A wasted opportunity. He had at least two minutes to make an impact (that's a full minute and a half more than Dave Trott ever got), to communicate his offer and persuade her to think of him first in the future, and he managed to fail on all three. Now let's look at the new story we created and see how that delivers the impact, communication and persuasion:

1 **Impact:** life-changing event – leaving job.

2 **Communication:** in the business of PR, events and entertainers.

3 **Persuasion:** 'Here's my card. Take it.'

Telling your story is about celebrating all the different stuff that you do, because not only will that make you memorable, but your story is why people want to hire or work with you. It will differentiate you from the competition. Tom Hulme, Design Director at IDEO, told us:

I have a weird background; it's eclectic, and that differentiates me. I'm conscious of the fact that my experiences carved and formed how I now think and that's actually only served to differentiate me, which feels more and more important to people.

So, like Tom, you need to think what differentiates *you*. There is no excuse for just being the same as everyone else. Both of us happen to have quite a weird set of experiences, like Tom; and we use those sets of experiences to differentiate ourselves from our competition. And guess what? It makes a good story.

If you're still thinking to yourself 'I simply have no story, just a bland series of events', don't worry. The story is in you. Trust us; it just needs teasing out. It is not unusual for those closest to the story (you) not to be able to see it. It's why people who have everything sometimes end up depressed; they can no longer see they have everything. It's why successful people feel as though they have failed; they are so close to the success that they cannot view through the eyes of others. And it's why pretty people think they are ugly; they only focus on the thing that they don't like, which is usually the one thing everyone loves. So, if you believe that your story has no impact, has nothing to communicate and little to persuade people with, relax: we have a solution.

To find out more about you and bring out the story you will need to start by asking people close to you for help. Ask them these questions:

1   If you needed to introduce me to someone, and you wanted to impress them, what would you say?

2   Name one thing about me that makes me stand out.

3   Why would you buy from me?

Ask this of a few people who know you well and whom you trust. Don't be shy to explain that for your mash-up career to be a success you need to make an impact, communicate what you do and persuade people to buy your service. Be clear of your reason for asking, and that way friends will be able to answer in a way that empowers your story. Take all your answers and stick them up on a wall: all the impact answers, all the communication answers and all the persuasion answers. If you struggle to see the obvious story, call back your friends and ask them to help you identify the most impactful statement and best communication. Your persuasive element will come naturally as a closing statement to what it is you are communicating. Now that you have the bare bones of your story you just need to link it together to make it flow.

All this work will go a long way to creating your image, creating the right perception and making you famous. Every time you meet someone you are marketing yourself. Get over the stigma of self-promotion, and don't underplay your story. It's often all you have, so make it powerful. Don't hide your talents in those three words 'amongst other things', which reeks of lack of confidence in what you offer. Confidence goes a long way. It says silently to the recipient that you are practised, understand the subject, are passionate about it and can therefore deliver a good result. So what about when you walk into a room full of people and it feels as though everyone is better than you? Remember this: they are all just as nervous as you, only some of them are better at acting more confident. You're breaking the mould, daring to be comfortable in your own skin, working with what you have and recognizing what is good about that. So don't be shy – this is *you*.

What about telling your story online? Digital tools provide the opportunity to market your full talents cheaply and seamlessly. A website, a blog or Twitter will give your audience a true sense of the real you and all your incarnations in a natural way; if you tell your story online, people will get a sense about your personality and understand your plurality. The internet is a gift to the masher: it provides the platform to tell your story via words and pictures. You can pick whatever floats your boat: curate some ideas via Tumblr; post an online column with a blog; tell a story via Instagram or Flickr. David Hieatt leads a multidimensional work life as founder of the Do Lectures, alongside running a jeans company; the web is a great platform for telling his story. He told us:

I use the internet to tell the world. I am a storyteller. The internet tells stories well.

Never forget that you are your story, so telling your story is one of the most important considerations in communicating your multidimensional talents. Your story is a powerful tool that will act as your differentiator, will make the complicated simple and will make sense of all that wonderful, eclectic stuff you do in your life. Your story is how you can package it all up to make you gettable, so make sure it has impact, communicates and persuades.

Name: Alexia Leachman

Location: Nottingham, England

Twitter: @alexia1

Twitter Bio: "Mojo hunter & @head_trash clearer at @BBrands. Speaker & fast talker, spiritual being, harnesser of energy, lover of dirty beats & greedie French foodie"

1   **So tell us your multidimensional talents, how you earn a living.** I help people to clear their head trash and find their mojo. Essentially, this is predominantly about helping people to discover, define and refine their personal brands so they are better able to achieve what they set out to do. In order to be able to articulate who we are and what we do, we first have to understand and be clear about who we are and the value we offer others. I help businesses and people to figure this out. And if any head trash muddies the water, we clear that too!

The head trash clearance part of my work has now developed a life of its own and I have a lot of people approach me just for this. This led me to join forces with the guy that developed my favourite technique, reflective repatterning, and we now offer training in this technique to coaches, therapists, counsellors, body workers, etc. This might end up being a massive part of the business. Who knows?

Practically speaking, I do my work through working one to one with people (face to face and over Skype), delivering workshops and talks, and by selling digital products.

2   **When did you transition to go plural?** I quit my job as a brand marketer in the beauty industry four years ago and have been making the transition ever since. The transition has been slowed somewhat by life events, but I do feel that I have now made the full transition and everything seems to have fallen into place. I always knew that I would have a portfolio career, as I could see it coming as a trend a long time ago... I also knew that it would be a style that would suit me, as I love variety and get bored easily.

3   **What's your strategy for answering the 'What do you do?' dinner party/pub question?** I ask questions before getting pinned down on this. What I do is perceived differently depending on who's receiving it, what their needs are, and how I might work with them, so I try to get as much info about them first so that I can tailor my response and ensure it's relevant to them. I have several snappy/short responses that trigger the response 'Ooh! That sounds interesting. What's that? How do you do that?' that kick-starts a conversation. I try to use language that is memorable and compelling and that people are likely to remember that will lead them to me if they google those words and/or my name. I also always share stories of success, ie how I've worked with someone else like them and what their challenge was and what the outcome was... I make sure that this story *is* a story and full of colour, adventure and emotion. I want to engage their emotions when I share what I do.

4 **How do you sell your multidimensional talents?**
I use social media a lot (Twitter, YouTube, Facebook,
Foursquare, Instagram, LinkedIn) to ensure I remain
front of mind in a relevant way. I can't guarantee that
this is effective, but it seems to be working so far. I also
blog on my own sites as well as for other high-traffic
sites.

In the real world I do talks and events. I network and
will happily meet with anyone who I feel would be
worth linking up with, no matter how random it might
appear. I regularly touch base with people that I know
and keep them updated in a non-salesy way (I hope!)
on what I'm up to.

5 **What are the joys of a work life where you mash up
different talents?** Flexible to work on my terms with
people who energize me, or those who I know I can
really help and add value to. I don't consider what I do
to be work… It's what I love doing and that's it. I love
variety and I love the fact that each day is different and
who knows what skills or challenges I may be faced with.

6 **And what are your pain points in doing more than one
thing?** I'm full of ideas and it's hard putting some of
them aside and knowing which ones to focus on. I've
always had to juggle lots of projects in my work as a
marketer, so I'm used to having lots on the go, and this
is my modus operandi. Also, because I have so many
things on the go, I find it hard to switch off. I'm usually
too excited to get to sleep! But I prefer that than being
stressed like I used to be in my previous jobs.

SO WHAT IS THE TRICK
TO SELLING YOUR MULTIPLE
SKILLS SUCCESSFULLY?
SETTING UP YOUR MASH
STALL SO YOUR OFFERINGS
ARE COMPELLING AND
GETTABLE.

10

How to sell your multiple offerings

So what is the trick to selling your mash successfully, to making your fortune by doing more than one thing? The answer is about being focused on what the client (for 'client' also think employer, boss, customer or audience) wants, *not* trying to sell someone the different strings of your bow for the sake of it. Setting up your mash stall is about listening to what the client wants and then boxing out your talents and services into a compelling, *gettable* package.

Throughout our respective careers we've met a couple of hundred business owners, entrepreneurs and CEOs. We've drunk gallons of tea and coffee at meetings where we have listened to common and familiar problems of businesses needing help: needing help fine-tuning their product or service; needing help keeping costs down; needing help standing out from the crowd. And many times we've both felt, well, we can help them with all that. Every single one. We sometimes feel like the kid in class, ever keen, sticking his hand up saying 'Yes, I can do that, miss.' Getting your sell right so you're not looking like the overzealous schoolkid is a delicate balancing act. It relies on trusting your instinct, being on the right wavelength, being tuned in to what your client needs and amplifying the appropriate talents.

So consider this. You're going in to have an introductory chat with a client tomorrow, or maybe you're going to meet a potential new employer to tell her why you'd be a great new hire. In both cases you've already heard her pain points and your head is swimming with ideas of how you could help her business. You're meeting for coffee at 2 pm, and you will wow her with all the various things you can do for her. From strategy to fulfilment to helping her staff get in the correct mindset: you'll be her one stop shop to help get her business back on track or to supply that service or sell that product. *Stop!*

Going into that meeting and saying you can do everything under the sun is a risky strategy. Why? Because that business owner is only human, and she'll be sceptical that you can really do everything. Or she'll hear you out over coffee and then later on scratch her head and ponder 'What exactly was that person saying? How could that person help me again?'

It's a lesson both of us have learnt in our career. So the first step in selling your plural talents is to discover your client's pain point and give her a focused solution of how you can solve it for her. Setting out your stall so that you are recognized as the person who solves her problem, removes the headache and fills that vacuum will be memorable. Once you're in the door and the client is loving your solution, then – and only then – you introduce her to more of your skills. Selling starts by viewing your approach through the lens of the buyer.

Your client has in her head a problem that exists in a department of the business. That is her focus; it is holding her attention and she is looking for someone who can solve her problem. If you have a leak in your house you probably want to hire a plumber, not a decorator who can also fix pipes. But, if the plumber's good and tells you he originally trained as a decorator and still does the occasional job, he might be a good, safe pair of hands to do that painting. But the single skill, that laser-focused one, that is what penetrates the barriers, beats off the competition and gets you through the door. Think of it as the Trojan horse; once you are through the walls of the castle, then you reveal all your other talents and skills.

It is important to listen first to clients' problems, really understand what it is that is keeping them up at night, because that is the stuff they will pay for today. Far too many people go in all guns blazing with a list of solutions they have to offer in the hope that one of them will resonate with the client. At best the client thinks you are brilliant but far too talented to solve her problem; at worst your list of skills ends up fogging the client's mind. There is a better way. First ask what it is the client needs. That sounds easy, but how do you ask such a probing question of a client or employer?

You would think that a client would want to tell you first, but this is often not the case for so many reasons. Clients may be too close to the problem; they just know something is not right with the business and it needs fixing. They may not be able to articulate the problem, or they may simply be polite and willing to 'hear you out' first.

Now business problems are like little children: they can sneak up behind you unnoticed, they have sudden growth spurts, and they can go nuclear at the most inappropriate times. So the average client has most likely gone to a meeting that morning and heard for the first time that this new problem exists, gone to lunch and come back to find it has escalated and the promised solutions are not working. Then the client sits down for coffee with you with a head swimming in problems, half-thought-out solutions and a bunch of 'notes to self'. And you wonder why 10 minutes into the meeting the client loses eye contact and seems to drift off? You know that feeling, right? You are speaking to clients and suddenly it's like they are not in the room any more. Was it something you said? Did you spark an idea? Are you boring them? You need to fish out of their heads the issue that is most problematic to them, because that is the one they will most definitely pay for someone to solve.

So over coffee at that first meeting, don't start with the 'Let me tell you about myself' routine. Instead first ask about the client's career, role and business. Effectively selling your mash starts with *listening*, so ask questions and then sit back and listen carefully.

Understanding clients' careers or back stories will give you a clue to where they have come from and where they are likely to want to go next. Understanding a client's business will give you insight as to where and how you must fit in.

At times, you may struggle to get clarity from the other side of the coffee table. She may be vague, so here is a simple yet effective question to yield some clarity: 'If you woke up tomorrow morning and everything in your business was just the way you wanted it to be what would be different?' This question forces her to think of the business problem, invites her to explain what the solution would look like, and potentially gets her visualizing the problem solved with you as part of the solution. Now you know the client's problem you can finally start telling her all about your skills, right?

Once you have that clarity of the headache that needs fixing, it is your turn to offer your solution. Rather than just dive in and say 'I'm your person', use these three steps to best position yourself and your talents:

→ **Step one:** Acknowledge that you have solved a similar problem for a similar type of client in the past, thus establishing that you have previous experience in that field.

→ **Step two:** Bring to life the results you achieved for your previous client, especially if you have any actual figures.

→ **Step three:** Make it clear how to hire you.

This clarity will mean that your offer will remain firmly in the mind of the client for the day.

Ian tried out this new script in his own business development. Instead of 'I can do that', he now says 'I've done a very similar project and the results were...' It isn't a hollow promise; it is a factual statement that he has done something similar before and therefore has experience in that field. Once Ian establishes his experience he then needs to qualify why the client should hire him. To do this Ian describes the problem his client had and how he solved it for the client and then closes with the outcome of working with the client, the all-important measurable result.

Plucking achievements from your own story and career and using them as proof of ability are much more powerful than promising 'I can do that.' Of course, you will need to be able to provide credible evidence of what you can do based on what you have done, including for example case studies, testimonials and other proof of results. Take this into consideration with the work you are doing now; make sure you are gathering all the facts, feedback and great comments that you can use to showcase your abilities to the next client.

Then your sell will be quick, compelling, businesslike, buyable and memorable. No 20-slide presentation, no big pitch, just the simple ability to articulate back to the potential client their particular problem, your experience of solving a similar problem and the result. It's much more powerful to understand their single most pressing need and answer it with a compelling story. When they hire you, then you will have plenty of time later to drip-feed them with more of your skills. It's important that you package up all your past projects so when required you can instantly produce the most fitting example. A mistake people make is that they tell their whole story the moment they meet a potential client. Yes, they do have multiple skills, but they tend to lack one important one, the ability to listen.

If you're lacking the confidence when facing a potential client or prospect, why not try embracing the spirit of the blag. What is the spirit of the blag? The spirit of the blag is a wonderful thing. It has all the energy required to get things moving in the right direction, but it should not be muddled up with plain old blagging, which is of course making things up to get what you want. For example, blagging your way into the VIP enclosure by name-dropping is not what we're talking about. But look at those valuable attributes that you could bring to bear on your prospect meeting: the swagger and the self-belief that all go towards projecting confidence. If you know what you are doing but lack the glow of confidence the client will probably sense that and go elsewhere. That spirit of the blag, that confidence that makes you walk taller, is important in securing your new job or next gig. Knowing that people want to hire those who can solve the kind of problem that they have means you need to project that by appearing confident. If you haven't got the belief in yourself that you can pull this off then no one else will have it in you.

Along with that new-found sense of confidence, remember to keep your message simple and focused. The saying goes: Throw me a ball and I will catch it. Throw me 12 balls all at the same time and I may be able to catch two; the other 10 will end up on the floor. So your message on your initial introduction must be single-minded in order that it doesn't end up on the floor. It's no good just rattling off a list of 12 different things you can offer if 10 will be missed. It is Sod's Law that skill number nine is the one they are after, and there it is lying on the floor. Categorizing all your skills in the recipient's mind in one dash will be too much effort. So you need to identify prospects' requirements and then create a place in their minds so they can easily choose you.

Effectively selling your multidimensional talents to a client or employer starts with listening. Then respond with a laser-focused offering that acts as your Trojan horse for getting in the door. Finally you'll need to box up your offering into something more tangible that they actually want to buy.

Name: Melissa Pierce

Location: Chicago

Twitter: @melissapierce

Twitter Bio: "Pro Mess Anti Crap. Creator of award winning film series Life In Perpetual Beta and hundreds of other less well known good ideas"

1 **So tell us your multidimensional talents, how you earn a living.** On my business card, my talents include being a film-maker, a risk taker and a fun maker. I earn my living doing all three of those in one fashion or another, usually just juggling projects. Often times, I'm hired to showcase my own personality, with one of these three talents as the tie-in to whomever I'm hired to work for.

2 **When did you transition to go plural?** My transition has always been plural, but I did get tired of having separate business cards for each venture, which is why I combined them into one card.

3 **What's your strategy for answering the 'What do you do?' dinner party/pub question?** The easier 'What do you do?' answer for me is to say 'I am a film-maker, a risk taker and a fun maker, and I use my creative talents to make this world a cooler place to live.' I find this is not only vague enough that people continue to ask questions, but also sets me apart as someone with multidimensional talents that are worth discovering. It makes me hard to define and keeps me an 'interesting' conversationalist.

4 **How do you sell your multidimensional talents?** I am a big proponent of being as upfront as possible when selling my talents, and am ever grateful for networking events and social media. It's easy for me to ask if

someone needs a camera person, or to point people to the various computer programming classes I organize, or my latest event project, without turning people off. What's great about being multidimensional and not concentrating on just one area of expertise is that people are more forgiving of me telling them about what I'm doing. They feel it's not selling but more of a buffet of awesomeness to choose from.

5 **What are the joys of a work life where you mash up different talents?** I love that every separate project I work on feeds into other projects. A satire video piece I shoot may dovetail nicely into an event I'm coordinating, and both of them might be perfect to promote a new venture I'm involved in. I like that, by leaving my creativity unboxed, I am able to incorporate all the moving pieces, that I have created a niche for myself that is focused in every direction.

6 **And what are your pain points in doing more than one thing?** My family can no longer explain exactly what I do to anyone, and my résumé looks a mess. I often say that I am 'unemployable' in a traditional office setting because I would disrupt the very linear way business is traditionally done. *That* is a pain point. Being my own boss and already having so many strings to hold on to, I have to also hold the string of caring for my financial future. I can't fall back on my employer's cushy pension plan. I have to think about that for myself.

MASHING IS NOT ABOUT
'ALL OR NOTHING' CHOICES;
YOU DON'T HAVE TO QUIT
YOUR DAY JOB – YOU CAN
DEVELOP A HOBBY BUSINESS
IN YOUR SPARE TIME.

11

Your ideas lab

Mashing is not about 'all or nothing' choices; you don't have to quit your day job – you can develop a hobby business in your spare time. In the old days if people wanted some extra cash or stimulation they did part-time jobs in the evening – working a shift in a pub or waiting tables. Now people run businesses! All they need is an idea, a commitment to make it work and some raw materials.

We met Michael Mentessi, an enterprising young guy who'd read our last book, *Zoom! The Faster Way to Make Your Business Idea Happen*. Realizing that his current day job is not what he wants to do for the rest of his life, Michael started a weekly 'Ideas Club' at work where he and his co-workers develop business ideas. Michael told us he's currently developing two very different projects: a smartphone app and a croissant baking business. For Michael it's all about doing it on the side, gaining confidence and finding out what works. He has created the time to experiment with different business ideas. What a great idea. Could you set up an Ideas Club in your kitchen, local pub or office?

You might be reading this thinking you don't have enough time to add a side project. All the usual reasons: you're flat out with your day job; you have a family; you need time to unwind after work. Come on, look at how you really spend your spare time. TV? Facebook? Pub? Not many things in life are equal, but we all have the same amount of time, rich or poor, fat or thin, young or old: 24 hours of it every day. It's up to us how we choose to use that time. If you were to view time as a precious commodity not to be wasted what would you do less of and what would you do more of? The choice is yours. More reality TV peppered with commercials, more status updates, or would you choose real fulfilment from the possibilities that a side project brings? Procrastination isn't just your enemy; it is everyone's. But right now you – and only you – have the power to choose how you best spend your time. Start to look around you: what is productive and what is a mere distraction? What is saving you time and what is eating away at your time? Your mobile phone does not save you time if you spend hours replying to mindless text messages. Your iPad does not save you time if its main function is to provide the platform for Angry Birds. Your laptop does not save you time if you sit in front of it watching the status bar fill up as you download your next movie. Most of us get so skilled at wasting time that we can do it brilliantly without ever consciously thinking about it. So how can you overcome the problem of living a life where spare time has become hijacked?

It all begins by taking stock of your time, just as you would any other precious commodity that you value. To achieve that you are going to audit your time. It's easy, it will be a revelation and, what's more, it is empowering. For the next eight days you will keep a record of where your time is going. This record will be a realistic reflection of how your time is used. So, if you're scratching your head wondering how you have time for a side project, we challenge you right now to do this for the next eight days. Take a piece of plain paper and fold it into quarters. You now have four squares on each side. Carry this paper with you for the next eight days. In each of the boxes write down what you spend your time doing. So why eight days and not a convenient seven-day week? What will be interesting is to see if the very act of noting where your time is going creates a change in your behaviour on the eighth day. Is day eight a repeat of day one, or does seeing where you are wasting time create a change?

Here's an example of how the first day may look:

Monday

7.50	*Wake up/get ready*
8.30	*Travel*
9–5.45	*Work*
5.45	*Travel*
6.15	*Supermarket*
7.00	*Cook and eat*
8.30	*TV/film*
10.30	*Washing-up*
11.00	*Check e-mail (and other computer-related distractions)*
12.00	*Bed*

Looking at the Monday example you can see that watching TV could be replaced by a side project task; swap the supermarket for a weekly food delivery. And ask yourself: do you really need to check your e-mail at 11 pm? If you could get to bed an hour earlier you could get up an hour earlier. Are we sounding a bit harsh? Too bad. If you want to make real change then you will need to be harsh. The good news is that often when we see how we are using our time in black and white we are able to make changes, small ones at first, but nonetheless significant. So could your new agenda look like this?

7.00	*Wake up/get ready*
7.40	*Work on my own project*
8.30	*Travel*
9–12	*Work*
12–1	*Lunch (work on my own project)*
5.30	*Travel*
6.00	*Cook and eat*
7.30	*Unwind TV*
8.00	*Work on my own project*
11.00	*Set goals for following day*
11.30	*Bed*

Four hours and 50 minutes of time recovered. You could really move a side project forward or learn a new skill with that much additional time.

We interviewed Shane Mac, the Seattle-based masher, who lists more than 18 different strings to his bow on his website. He told us:

I believe what you do on the side will create your next job or promotion. The skills you gain while working on your own things should benefit your skills you need to excel in your full-time job. Sometimes it may even create your full-time job. I think the future is about multiple skills and streams of income, not one. It may be the way of the post-industrial revolution... I'd bet on it.

Shane made a nice little video that's worth checking out, and even better it will take only 129 seconds to watch (see http://tinyurl.com/mashshane).

Although a side project might start outside of the nine-to-five, it can actually then become part of the job itself as you use the side project to carve a new role. On *the99percent.com* website, Jake Cook tells the story of Ben Barry, a designer at Facebook who created a great side project: setting up a screen-printing studio in the company's warehouse. Although he started designing and printing posters at weekends and evenings, this ended up being part of his actual job, resulting in him producing posters and print materials for President Obama's visit to Facebook:

> **Now it makes up a big part of my job, even though nobody asked me to do it and it's not what I was originally hired to do. I didn't ask for permission, I just did it.**
>
> **(the99percent.com)**

Ben used his side project to prove that he could create great print work; then when his employers saw the results he was encouraged to bring it in-house as part of his job. Ben added:

> **You have to make those opportunities happen and take those risks.**

The side project has the potential for you to test, trial and prototype ideas without the risk of sacrificing your main income. Sometimes the first thing you try may not be a success. It may prove that what you thought would be a good idea turns out to be the exact opposite. That's OK. It's worth remembering that Thomas Edison failed at inventing the light bulb 10,000 times. His persistence paid off. So don't give up the race because you fell over once. This is not a 100-metre sprint; this is a lifestyle choice that will play out over the rest of your life. If your first idea doesn't work, take a deep breath, learn from what went wrong and continue.

That sense of persistence is important, because the side project is a canvas on which you can experiment, play, even mess around; it won't always happen overnight. As the artist, writer and blogger Austin Kleon reminds us:

> It's the side projects that blow up. By side projects I mean the stuff that you thought was just messing around. Stuff that's play. That's where the magic happens.

Austin believes that, by keeping the side project as just 'play', it can be more powerful in informing new directions and ultimately new revenue streams. But it is important to stand back from this 'play on the side' and see how it can be turned into real cash. Certainly, you might be enjoying what you are doing, but you are missing a trick by not turning it into cash.

You may be sceptical about trying to make money through a hobby, ie something that is only connected with pleasure. Making cash from what you love may seem brash. But pause before you dismiss your hobby as the route to a second income. Consider the people you could help who share your passion, the extra connections it could bring you or the deeper understanding of your subject that may be realized. We decided to write about turning your hobby into another string to your bow for one reason. There is no bigger motivator than pleasure, so if you wanted to create a low-risk business on the side then your hobby, your passion or your pleasure is a great place to start.

Recently we were at a motor racing event. Most of the drivers were wealthy amateurs who raced for pleasure. We noticed that the photographers present were often asked by the drivers if they had any good photos of them and their cars. Conversations would follow as a driver described a car, the photographer fumbled with the camera and both parties squinted at a tiny screen on the back of the camera to try to assess if the photo was right. How easy would it be for the photographer to post the photos on a blog as low-resolution pictures and let the drivers order high-resolution versions? After all, motor sport is not cheap, and the guy asking for photos was racing his highly expensive Bentley Continental GT Speed; we're convinced he would happily pay for a sharply focused photo that captured him racing his pride and joy. The photographer has already invested in thousands of pounds' worth of camera kit. Why not another £10 on business cards directing drivers to a blog to view the photos? Come on, it's not rocket science, is it?

Don't underestimate the potential of what you can do on the side. This is your playing field, your blank canvas, your lab – to innovate, experiment, just try stuff out and see what works. Your only risk? That you missed a TV show or didn't see that Facebook status update. Whether it is shaping your next career move, creating some extra cash or learning something new, do it on the side.

Name: Tom Alcott	
Location: Bristol	
Twitter: @Tom_Alcott	
Twitter Bio: "SNA, Pepper & Charity Water. That's me in a peppery, watery, networky nutshell. See also www.peppermongers.co.uk & www.frankwater.com"	

1   **So tell us your multidimensional talents, how you earn a living.** I do three things: I run a consultancy doing social network analysis, I run the retail division of a water charity and I run a spice trading company. On the surface they all appear very different things but actually there are a lot of commonalities. It started with the social network consultancy and that was quite successful, so I was going to gift money to charity but decided instead to set up my own charity, FRANK Water. That grew from one project to 100 projects running in India. Whilst visiting FRANK Water projects in India I came across the pepper spices on plantations and I saw a business opportunity there. They all evolved out of each other. Right now I earn my income from all three companies, but FRANK Water is not-for-profit, donating 100 per cent of its profit to the charity.

2   **When did you transition to go plural?** About 10 years ago a good idea randomly presented itself. You either seize that idea or you do not. In the last 10 years a couple of good ideas came up and I seized them. I try to develop them rapidly, because that is one of the few strengths of being a small business – reacting quickly.

3 **What's your strategy for answering the 'What do you do?' dinner party/pub question?** I just say I am a spice trader. If I say I am a social network analyst you get two responses. Eyes glaze over, you get a tumbleweed moment, they don't understand what you do and they feel awkward. Secondly, if you say that you're a social networks analyst they may think that they understand what you do, but they don't. They think you are into Facebook and Twitter.

FRANK Water is slightly complicated; it's funding clean water projects in India, and most people don't understand India, so you end up in a political argument about how generally ignorant we are of poverty and the causes of poverty.

Everyone knows what a peppercorn is, and no one has ever met a peppermonger before. That makes it interesting. It's a bit like meeting an astronaut; everyone is immediately interested. Pepper is my focus today and will be for the next two years as I launch the company, so I introduce myself as a peppermonger and may add that I work for a charity too.

4 **How do you sell your multidimensional talents?** I don't really sell them as much as leverage them. So I use my deep understanding of social networks to leverage social media for FRANK Water. Then I use the knowledge I have gained from FRANK Water, such as distribution, supply chain, getting products in stores, to launch peppermongers.

The common thing across all this is running a small business, and you need two separate skills to run a business: the administration and the product. You need to be on top of PAYE, cash flow and VAT, but you also need to be the best at what you do.

5   What are the joys of a work life where you mash up different talents? In a small way you can control your own destiny. So I would say control, although to be honest you are out of control most of the time, so perhaps it is the illusion of control that is the joy.

6   And what are your pain points in doing more than one thing? There is only one thing worse than a to-do list and that is three to-do lists. It is all about prioritizing, and it changes daily. You may sit down to do a day of peppermonger work and a crisis appears in the consultancy; then you may sit down to do FRANK Water work and a big order comes in for peppercorns that needs fulfilling immediately.

I am also at risk of having another idea. If another idea bubbles up I will have a dilemma: do I go for that idea or pass it? Because I am meeting so many interesting people I run the risk that during the conversation another idea presents itself in the mash and I may feel compelled to follow it up.

HOW TO ADD MORE SELLABLE TALENTS BY FINDING YOUR BY-PRODUCTS.

12

Adding a new string to your bow

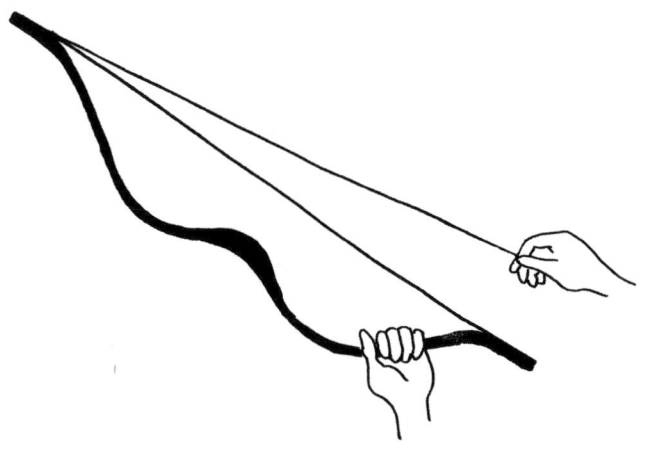

The joy of mashing is that there are no limits to what you can and can't do. If you spot a trend in the marketplace and know you can fill a niche by serving it, or you just decide you want to do more, you can add another string to your bow. Adding a new string to your bow can be achieved by discovering your by-products. Adding one skill to another may actually result in a third, or a fourth, skill.

So where to start with adding a new string to your bow? Sometimes we add strings by default, because we have to. Technology has forced many of us to add new strings or, if not, face extinction by being left behind. You don't see many designers today who are just graphic designers, creating work only for print; their skills are transferable, so they have followed the work and now they also design for online. It might not be a voluntary move, but it's probably a necessary one. The same with a writer, who becomes a content creator, as she doesn't just write newspaper articles or brochure copy, but also writes blog posts and grabs content on video. These by-products have been forced by technological change.

Other by-products arise from the necessary self-sufficiency of the one-person business. The one-person business has become adept at doing everything from actually delivering the product or service to selling, marketing and administering. Again, this becomes a by-product, as people can offer their know-how to other people in their sector via how-to guides and training courses. Many people who were the early adopters in the digital world and saw the benefits of social media have become social media trainers themselves as a by-product of their experience.

If you're struggling to work out your by-product, consider how Jason Fried thinks of it. Jason is founder of the Chicago-based software business 37signals, whose by-products (training classes, books, speaking engagements) have become as important revenue generators as the core business itself. He describes your by-product as sweeping up the sawdust and making it into something else sellable. So what is the sawdust that comes from creating your own product or service? Is it know-how? Is it another trade?

Meet Richard, a successful copywriter. So what's his by-product? Teaching others how to write. Richard now runs workshops for clients in the United Kingdom and United States; it's a great example of a lucrative by-product, as he can charge more per day training clients than he can writing copy. Teaching is a good by-product; it's what artists have done for decades, but it applies to other areas as well, whether you're a coffee shop barista or an accountant.

Maybe you are thinking that you can't start selling that additional skill until you have the certificate to prove it? This may be true if your new skill is dentistry or architecture, where fundamental knowledge is required to avoid pain and destruction. But, for lots of new strings, good enough is good enough, and you'll be measured on your ability and results, not on a paper qualification.

Our friend Matt is a well-respected freelance TV sound recordist who works on some of the biggest shows around: *The X Factor* and *Britain's Got Talent*. But he also happens to be a rather good photographer and videographer. Recently Matt had an opportunity to add a string to his bow when the TV company wanted to try out a new camera technology. Matt happened to have the kit they needed and offered to lend it and operate it for them. Subsequently they gave him paid work as the camera operator, which turned out to be more lucrative, especially as he's hiring them his kit too. Being able to offer a mixture of jobs has made him more valuable to his client, plus he's getting offered more days' work as a result. Matt fast-tracked a new string to his bow without going through the 'Look at me, I have completed this course, so I must be good' training. It's an emerging technology, and he knew how it worked. He was in the right place at the right time. He did not ask them to wait three months whilst he took lessons to gain a certificate. He took the opportunity and the challenge to pursue something he loved, and in doing so he added another skill, another revenue stream and another reason to smile.

If you think you can do it – and you're good at it – then that is possibly all you need to start trading. But when is good enough good enough? We have met too many people who believe that until they are noted as experts then they could not possibly charge for the value they can add. That mindset will slow you down and cost you money. You need to change to a mindset that recognizes the moment that you start creating value and charging for that added value.

The carpenter who built a friend's wardrobes confessed that he had no official qualification as a carpenter, but learnt his skills from his father, who loved working with wood, creating lines that are true and seeing people's ideas realized. Was the carpenter good? Yes. Was he a 10 out of 10? Our friend had no idea. As the proud owner of well-fitted wardrobes he couldn't honestly tell you the difference between an 8 and a 10. If you currently rate yourself at 8 out of 10 for aptitude, you could complete a one-year course and invest £3,000 and your time, and it might take you to 9.5. The question is: will the marketplace really notice that extra 1.5 out of 10? Will it make a difference? Yep, probably not.

But if you're scratching your head and struggling to identify exactly what that new string to your bow could be, you need to take time out, press the pause button and stand back. Every six months, review what's in the mix. Pressing pause could be taking time out from the day-to-day to sit on the beach or stroll through a city, reflecting on what you have achieved and pondering where you may want to go in the future. This break from the regular work will give you the space to let new thinking happen. Once you have reflected on what you have been doing you will be able to ask the questions:

1 What have you wanted to do but not tried?

2 Where is there untapped potential?

3 What else could you offer?

When you create time just to think about the future you will get some very interesting answers – not the kind of thoughts you would have if you were busy taking calls, fulfilling on projects or chasing new business. With a couple of days just to think and a notepad to jot down the ideas you will be able to get a clear vision of what you really want.

Like many women in a similar position, Ian's wife Zoë took the opportunity of having kids to press that pause button and review what she wanted to do.

She decided to train as a hypnotherapist, qualifying two years later. She loved that experience, but still had an artistic yearning deep inside her. The therapy was going to stimulate her, but what about her artistic streak? So when Ian and David's last book, *Zoom!*, needed some doodles, Ian suggested Zoë do them. 'But I'm not a doodler', she replied. 'But you can be, just by doing it. By doing it, you've become it', Ian replied, and by the end of that evening the doodles were shaping up and being scanned and sent over to David. You can see them in the book. By thinking plural, not singular, she did not have to make crude black or white choices; she instead can be truly multicoloured. It took a little time and persuasion for Zoë to believe that she could be the hypnotherapist as well as the doodler, but once she accepted that we can wear more than one label she felt comfortable with it and able to include it in conversation. Taking time to press pause enabled Zoë not just to explore a new direction with hypnotherapy but also to add another string to her bow that she could have easily missed.

You just have to use your Lego skills. Watch any child playing with Lego bricks, building a tower higher and higher, but getting frustrated when it collapses. To avoid the collapse you need to make each layer stable before adding the next, pushing down on the bricks, making sure they are all fully pressed to the one below. When you build your mashed-up life, try thinking like a Lego builder. Start a layer at a time, making sure the foundation of your career is stable before you build the next on top of it. Frances Booth started offering the photography services only once the writing part of her business was stable. That is, she only added another string to her bow once she was totally adept at writing and that was generating enough revenue. Until that point the photography remained a hobby. Once the foundation – that first layer of Lego bricks – was stable and firm, then (and only then) she built on it. So the foundation should be your primary skill. It could be writing or designing or finance or web developing. On top of that you add your new layers, one at a time. The base may be what people know you best for, or what you've spent most of your life doing, or perhaps what earns you the most money. Work out what your foundation layer is, and then go and add your new strings to your bow one layer at a time.

If you're looking to add another string
to your bow, if you've spotted
an opportunity that is a natural
by-product of your know-how, if you
know you can provide value and
know-how to an employer or client,
then that is enough. Forget the training
course, forget the certificate and just
get on and do it. Start doing it and
see if people will pay you for it.
Just go for it...

Name: Zoë Howe

Location: Essex, England

Twitter: @zoehowe

Twitter Bio: "Music writer, drummer, broadcaster, Scorpio"

1 So tell us your multidimensional talents, how you earn a living. By metaphorically spinning plates! I write music books, band bios and sleeve notes, and I am also the editor of the *Iceland Music Export* website, which aims to do exactly that: export Icelandic music to the world! Book-wise I am currently working on a book about Florence and the Machine for Omnibus Press, who published my previous books *Typical Girls? The Story of the Slits* and *How's Your Dad? Living in the Shadow of a Rock Star Parent*. Also, *Looking Back at Me*, the 'fractured autobiography' I worked on with local legend Wilko Johnson (of Dr Feelgood, Ian Dury and The Blockheads fame), is coming out this year (Cadiz Music). I also occasionally play gigs as a drummer and make radio series about music. So, as I say, spinning plates!

2 When did you transition to go plural? I think, when you are freelance and connected to the arts, you naturally morph your abilities in different ways depending on what is required of you and what inspires you! I also think that, being part of the music industry, I naturally find I want to explore different routes and areas within the music world, as one strand relates to, and nourishes, another. Curiosity and versatility is vital, but so is focus of course... I started off as an actor. I come from a theatre family, so this was me since childhood really, but I always loved rock 'n' roll and writing, so I don't know why it didn't occur to me to do what

I now do earlier! I started writing professionally when I was about 24 (eight years ago) and it grew from there. I'd played drums, on the other hand, since I was about 12, but when I was in my early twenties I took a hiatus, only picking up sticks again to mime in a Kelly Osbourne Doritos commercial when I was about 22! When I wrote the Slits book, however, I found myself inspired to play again, and I was fortunate enough to start playing with Viv Albertine, as she'd just picked up her guitar again after about 25 years away from it! So it was great fun and a real learning curve to play and record percussion and drums and also provide backing vocals for her. This led to me working with Anne Pigalle, who spotted me at one of Viv's gigs, free improviser Steve Beresford and The Clash's Mick Jones amongst others. It's been great to explore different styles of music – most recently I was playing with Southend voodoobilly band The Voronas, very different music again!

3   **What's your strategy for answering the 'What do you do?' dinner party/pub question?** It's a difficult one, but generally I just tell people that I write about rock 'n' roll and also play the drums. That tends to cover it neatly.

4   **How do you sell your multidimensional talents?** Social media is absolutely essential – it's a great way to keep people abreast of the different things that are going on – and keeping an updated website so people have a one-stop site to refer to if they want a general overview. Every day I bless Tim Berners-Lee for inventing the internet! It's an artist's best friend, and it's easier than ever to keep everyone informed, even for those of us who aren't naturally that great at pushing ourselves forward and blowing our own trumpets, as many artists are not. Those of us who

don't have managers need to be able to put themselves out there without feeling unduly uncomfortable about it, and social networking is a great way of doing that. On several occasions, just by writing something quirky and offhand like a blog post, I've been contacted by people who've become my future employers who've liked my writing style. So even when you don't think you're selling yourself, if it's online, you're selling yourself! So you have to be a bit careful what you write – you never know who's looking... It's also important to stay up to date with related events that are going on around you, to see where you or your product might tie in for some nifty cross-promotion!

5   **What are the joys of a work life where you mash up different talents?** I wouldn't have it any other way. It really is a joy, as you say. This kind of work life is always interesting and inspiring and often exciting, not least because it exposes me to so much music and culture that I might not have otherwise experienced, and brings me together with some wonderful people who I wouldn't necessarily have met. And, as I say, one thing tends to feed the other.

6   **And what are your pain points in doing more than one thing?** Sometimes it's difficult to focus – you can be concentrating so doggedly on one thing that you can miss something that could be really vital for something else that you're working on! Plus when you pour energy into one thing, you have a niggling guilt at the back of your mind that you should be spending time on the other! So it's really important to prioritize, particularly when you're on the brink of a larger-scale project like a book. I've improved a great deal on this! I used to stay up all night writing until I got tired. Now I set myself a routine and a daily word count, and can

work out how long it will approximately take me to complete the project as a result. I never go over this word count, even if I want to! There has to be time for resting, socializing, playing with the cat and watching *The Big Bang Theory*! It's very easy to become insular as a writer working from home. I feel very lucky that I can do that, but it can also turn one into a hermit! And part of the freelance life is meeting people, getting out there... They say 80 per cent of success is turning up! So discipline is really key, both in starting and seeing something through *and* knowing when to stop.

HOW BEING A MASTER OF
REINVENTION WILL SERVE
YOU WELL IN THIS PERIOD OF
RAPID CHANGE.

13

Reinvention time

If there's one certainty in this uncertain world it's that business is changing rapidly, and that speed of change isn't about to slow down, so your professional offering can't stand still. You need to keep pace with shifting trends, industry developments and client needs. Being a master of reinvention will serve you well in this period of rapid change, and in this chapter we will explain how you can be that master, how you can top up your skills and talents to fit those new demands, so if your current world gets saturated, stagnates or stalls you can stay ahead of the game.

Welcome to the rollercoaster career, where people – whether they're working for organizations or self-employed – don't stay in one role for long, constantly reinventing themselves, adding new strings to their bow with those inevitable ups and downs. For many in the job market, it won't be enough to offer just one skill any more; they'll have to embrace new ones both to remain employable and to stand out from the crowd. They'll need to become masters of reinvention, to take one career trajectory and turn it into a new one.

Have you ever stopped to think 'How on earth did I get to this point in my career?' Those career – and life – milestones are rarely the results of long, carefully crafted strategic plans and are more likely to be due to random serendipity and organic change. Morphing from one opportunity to another, stumbling across chance meetings, taking random turns off the main track: it's what we tend to do subconsciously all our lives. It's what we do on our journey through life as we reinvent ourselves from the classroom to the outside world. But that's where many of us stop. Right there. We get a job and we stick with it. And even if we don't stick to the same job or the same company, many of us opt to stay in the same kind of role, in the same kind of company. People do the same thing in finance, in sales, in operations. Despite the change they experienced in their earlier lives, as they get older they stick with the status quo. Change just seems to appear harder as you become an adult. But interestingly, for those who have seen the benefits of reinvention, would they ever opt to stand still again? Probably not. Especially when you consider all the new opportunities that are within your grasp. We are dynamic creatures living in dynamic times with the tools and intellect to create a dynamic life, and now another variable has entered the mix: suddenly what worked yesterday does not necessarily work today. Therefore we need to be ready to rethink and exploit our true dynamic abilities. You might instigate that reinvention, or more likely it will just happen as needs must be met. So why don't more people reinvent themselves?

Mainly because of fear: fear of losing status, fear of what others will say, fear of answering the 'What do you do?' question and of course the fear of failure. And in some cases, yes, it is true, the fear of success. Change always presents itself with risks, and with risk comes a level of fear. Although risk of failure is an obvious fear that we would wish to avoid, success has its own problems too. If you become successful you will change; you will become a different person, a successful person. You may outgrow friends; you will be open to new and probably bigger opportunities that you may feel compelled to explore, so you may move away from family. That creates fear, and especially in those close to you. Not out of malice, but for psychological reasons, those close to you may attempt to discourage you from reinventing yourself with comforting sayings like 'You should be grateful for what you have got.' But as our world rapidly changes you may find that you have no choice but to reinvent yourself.

Lynda Gratton of the London Business School says that the pace of change will be so rapid that people may have to acquire new expertise every few years if they want to be part of the lucrative market for scarce talent. Yes, it's about reinvention, and that is whether you're in a full-time job with the scope to reinvent yourself to survive, or in the open market and you need a new offering to earn money.

So there. Lynda has given you licence to explore your desire to deliver multiple skills. Your industry may be shrinking and you want to safeguard your income, your industry may be hit by an unlikely competitor, or you may simply have an 'itch you want to scratch', an interest in a new area.

Meet Hillman Curtis, a guy who spent his life embracing reinvention (Hillman sadly died in 2012). He was described by the *99percent* website as 'a decathlete of creative pursuits'. Hillman's career has embraced music, web design, writing and film. He taught himself web design when he got dropped by his record label, rose through the ranks at Macromedia working on flash design, and then developed film as a side project. He thrived on reinvention. He told Jake Cook:

I was given a lot of freedom growing up. My mother was an art teacher and never put a lot of pressure on me to pursue a particular path. I originally went to school for creative writing and film. I then spent

10 years pursuing music and after failing at that I did various random jobs. I got into design out of desperation – I didn't want to wait tables or pound nails again – without ever even having touched a computer.

(the99percent.com)

Being open to reinvention is about reconciling two – seemingly opposite – agendas. On the one hand you need to stay open to new areas you might want to explore, opportunities you spot, to see wherever the water flows. But on the other hand you must have a clear checklist to run every new opportunity by. Here is your three-point checklist to ensure your reinvention adds value:

1   What value will I get from this opportunity? Fun, fame or fortune? It doesn't have to be financial. It may be a great fun project, bring you fame in a new area of work like getting your foot in the door with a new client, getting an assignment that you can use to prove your competence, or it may be all about the new revenue stream.

2   How does it fit with my unifier (see Chapter 4)? This is key, because you need your plurality to have clarity. You don't want your working life to be a crazy mix of random stuff with no central theme. In Ian's case, this is about 'communicating ideas'; in David's case, it's about being a change agent. Those unifiers are broad enough to embrace a lot of plurality; they have a focus but not to the exclusion of everything else.

3 And a really simple question: does it play to my strengths? A really simple mantra for both our own work lives is 'Play where you play best.' So don't try to be good at something you're useless at.

By putting your reinvention past this checklist you can be sure you get the best chance of expanding your skills, staying employable and maintaining happiness.

Mike Southon told us:

> I can recommend reinventing yourself. For one thing, it is tremendous fun. I have variously been a chemical engineer, a computer training salesman, a spoof rock star, a salesman for hire, an author, a professional speaker and now a columnist. I have left out the adventures that went terribly wrong, of course, but it is all about the journey, not the destination.

Both of our respective careers have seen much reinvention. Was that reinvention strategic? Was it planned? Did we plot it on a path? Of course not. Like Mike Southon's journey, our career stepping stones from one thing to another have been a seemingly random bunch of experiences and roles led by curiosity, opportunity and, yep, pure luck and chance. The thing about reinvention is that you don't know what's next. It's being willing to embrace new thinking and new opportunities. So get ready to metamorphose to whatever's next.

Name: David Hieatt

Location: Cardigan Bay, Wales

Twitter: @davidhieatt

Twitter Bio: "Founder of Hiut Denim, Co-Founder of the Do Lectures"

1   So tell us your multidimensional talents, how you earn a living. I keep asking myself that. I put a Post-it note on the back of the door after I left howies. It said 'Create assets', and that is what I have been doing for the last two years. I started the Do Lectures, which I don't get paid by, but it helps me meet lots of amazing people, which is brilliant. It is good to do something for no return sometimes. It has given back to me many, many times.

I am about to start the Hiut Denim Co, which I am paid by. We will grow it into a small global denim company. Our town used to make 35,000 pairs of jeans a week, so the skills are here. That's helpful.

I also started a pub/restaurant called The 25 Mile. The main ingredients are sourced within a 25-mile radius as the crow flies. The aim is to do one so amazingly well that we end up doing 10 of them. In time, these assets will pay me back in money or make me feel proud. I get asked to do consultancy, but mostly I decline. I get asked to do talks; mostly I decline. I do a Do day course, 'How to build a brand with very little money', which I am paid for. That's about it.

2   When did you transition to go plural? I had a year where I wasn't allowed to start another clothing company, so I spent my time on the Do Lectures, and it kept tugging my heart. I had always wanted to do something world-class, and there it was right under my nose. Then a friend wanted to start a pub, and I said that wasn't a good idea. So I had an idea that local food is where the future lies for towns and communities. So I said yes, while I was waiting to be allowed to start my new jeans company. So plural came about from a non-compete clause in a contract. I will let you know if that was a good thing or not.

The thing that holds these things together is the town. Maybe a part of me wants to be successful for the town: to bring employment to it and to do things which change things – a town that is small but can learn not to play small.

3   **What's your strategy for answering the 'What do you do?' dinner party/pub question?** I am an entrepreneur. I am someone who is interested in how ideas change things. I like running companies, so that is what I do. I play at those things each day.

4   **How do you sell your multidimensional talents?** I just get on and 'start shipping' and see if there is a customer out there. I build things first and see if the phone rings. I use the internet to tell the world. I am a storyteller. The internet tells stories well.

5   **What are the joys of a work life where you mash up different talents?** I am obsessive, so it's good for me to spread that around. Otherwise I can get stuck in one groove. And I bring ideas from each thing. They all seem to feed into each other, which is good.

6   **And what are your pain points in doing more than one thing?** Time. But you have to split time up and keep to that discipline. It can work, but requires discipline.

HOW TO MAKE 1+1=3:
HOW YOUR MASH CAN BE GREATER THAN
THE SUM OF ITS PARTS.

14

The meaning of mash

The joy of mash is not just about having the freedom to involve yourself in different projects, wearing different hats in your job or running a hobby business in your spare time. No, the joy of mash is the value you get when you stir your talents into one multicoloured, mixed-up ball of Plasticine. One colour on its own would not be as nearly pleasing to the eye, but multiple swirling colours seamlessly bleeding into each other create beauty and elegance. When you combine your talents collectively, when they seamlessly bleed into each other so you create a new level of elegance, that creation is additional value you can offer, an additional value that is more than the sum of the parts. So how do you make 1+1=3?

Looked at individually your skills may appear random, but think how you can connect the dots to produce greater value. Look at how one skill directly influences another. It's not always obvious at first, but when you step back and view how your multiple skills influence everything you do you will realize that each skill adds greater value to the next. The net result of plugging one thing into another (or bunch of others) is powerful. Let's look at David's example first.

David's skills as a hypnotherapist can be more than just an interesting aside in a conversation. The skill brings a powerful added dimension to any discipline he plugs it into, making him a better change agent, a more effective creative director and an author with a difference. His work in therapy has taught him how to understand objections and lower barriers, which is very useful when he is working with teams or leading a project. His understanding of how the mind works means he is better placed to create real change. Also, his work in therapy requires him to think on his feet as he guides a client towards a solution in real time. That approach stretches David's creative abilities: very useful when you are challenged to generate new ideas. You can see how David's hypnotherapy strengthens other areas of his work.

Ian's collective talents similarly have value when added together. In his consultancy business, where he helps clients communicate their ideas, he devises strategies to stand out from the crowd; he's the client's go-to ideas guy. That's compelling, but the fact that Ian is also adept at writing means that he can take the idea to execution. Not having to hire a consultant and a writer as two separate people makes Ian a lot more valuable. Then his contacts in business journalism are valuable for telling client stories; additionally some of the people he's met as an author become guests for a radio show he contributes to. Success relies on that interrelationship; so long as he is open and transparent, everyone gains. The clients get more value and better results. Plurality wins!

Those learnings both of us apply from different parts of our mash – whether it's consultant, author or therapist – make us more innovative and effective at solving client problems, since the analogous worlds collide to help us solve challenges faster. So when you can cross borders from one discipline to another – having your feet planted in more than one world – the collective value tends to be greater than the sum of the parts. This is because one discipline can inform another. Our experience tells us that, by crossing these borders, the projects we are working on, the ideas we are devising or the books we are writing not only become more well rounded, but are likely to be more ground-breaking. So if you're talented at more than one thing and have interests in more than one area, you too may find the ideas you can produce have the power to be much more impactful than if you'd developed an idea in isolation as a specialist. Why? Because you are able to mix different ingredients, take inspiration from one area to add to another and produce the kind of results that a scientist in a white coat in a lab would never have come up with in 20 years of single, deep experimentation. That's because the scientist never thought to look outside the lab to see what was happening in the coffee shop, or to look up from the academic textbook and stare out of the bus window to get inspiration from the high street. The scientist missed out on that ability to apply that genius missing ingredient. In his manifesto 'The creative generalist: how broad thinking leads to big ideas', Steve Hardy suggested:

> Ideas cannot be limited to the confines of a silo. They need space to run around and occasionally bump into strangers.
>
> (Hardy, 2005)

Steve explains that ideas are the product of divergent thinking, dealing with completely unrelated notions. They come from 'a kaleidoscopic grab bag of other ideas'.

Apply that thinking to your mashed-up life, for the different elements of what you do, of your respective passions and interests, to bump into other different elements.

It's a lesson that Terence Conran is well aware of. Conran is the internationally renowned British designer who founded the Habitat retail store in the late 1960s. But there's more to Conran than that. As you enter The Way We Live Now exhibition at London's Design Museum (of which Conran is the founder) you're met with a cluster of six giant pencils leaning against the wall. Down the spine of each pencil is written one of the following roles: 'Designer', 'Retailer', 'Educator', 'Restaurateur',

'Maker', 'Entrepreneur'. Whilst these six roles are the respective strings to his bow, consider how his work has shaped contemporary lives: from the stuff that we have on our kitchen shelves to how design-savvy consumers have become. As a result of that collective contribution, Terence Conran has become a household name. He says:

> If offered something well designed, well made, of decent quality at a price they can afford, then people will like and buy it. This is the abiding principle to which I hold, whether as designer, retailer or restaurateur.

The value is in Terence's collective know-how: for example, he is able to deliver a better customer experience in his hotel or restaurants because his learnings as a designer mean he is sourcing chairs and tables that not only are comfortable and well designed but actually add value to the customer experience. Every aspect of the furnishings has been considered, from what they look like to the materials of construction and, critically, usability, all through the lens of a man who is expert in more than one thing: design, retail, restaurants and hospitality. It is Conran's personal unifier – as an arbiter of good taste – that he can bring to a restaurant, office redevelopment, product, clothing range, cars, consumer products and anything else he chooses to engage with.

So stand back and look at the collective power and value of the respective strings to your bow. See how you can multiply your different roles, passions and interests together to create something bigger than the sum of your parts. Explore how this makes you more of an asset in the marketplace, whether to a client or an employer. Think like Conran!

As soon as you realize that it is OK to do more than one thing then you will possibly find yourself doing more projects. Excitement is never far away for someone living the mash-up life, especially as you see how each string to your bow begins to influence the next, even if they are completely different types of projects with seemingly little or nothing in common. Ideas soon begin to flow between your projects. Working on one project may strike up an idea for a blog post for another, and during the writing of that post you may have a realization of how a third project can be improved. That constant flow between projects is not unusual; we are hearing it a lot. What you are not doing is spending an hour trying to solve a problem, completing that task and then starting on the next. Instead you work far more organically than that, so your two projects, although perhaps on the surface radically different in scope, begin to feel more like one. It gives you a wonderful sense of satisfaction when projects begin to bleed into each other, creating additional value. That's the story of our lives.

But it's not just combining project thinking to add value; what about connecting people and contacts from one of your worlds to another, and how it could bring huge value to you as the connector and huge value to them as the connected? Value to the connector may not necessarily come in the shape of an introduction fee or something you can monetize, but being seen as the person who can introduce and connect people from different worlds will be seen as a really valuable skill. When you are seen to be creating value everywhere then everything you do is seen as valuable. Great connectors whom we know just get a kick out of helping people by introducing them to others – the fact that it gives them pleasure is their motivator. Espree Devora is an internet entrepreneur in LA who is always going out of her way to send an e-mail to us or an introduction on Twitter to someone she thinks it would be helpful for us to meet. So get a reputation as a connector, introducing people across your mashed-up world. Spread good karma that way and you'll be rewarded in love, cash, kudos or beer.

Raj Dey, Founder and CEO of Enternships, also sits on the boards of other companies, and is a co-founder of StartUp Britain. Raj has found that having a diverse range of interests is really valuable, as he can cross-pollinate ideas and contacts. He told us:

 Having a quite eclectic mixture of activities ranging from charity and social enterprise space to also working with venture capital can cross-pollinate ideas and contacts.

He might go to a meeting with his start-up business hat on but find the meeting valuable for his charity interests. Success at mashing is about talking about all you do, as the multidimensional Gary Vaynerchuk reminds us:

> I think that every person is multidimensional and has enormous things they are good at and many different interests, and I think that the best way to communicate in this new social era is to talk about all of them; don't hide anything. Expand what you are talking about.

There is no set formula for maximizing your mash: it's about having the right mindset – allowing elements from one area to meld, inform and add value to another. It's stopping to think: how can that meeting I've just had add value to my other clients? How can that inspiring article I've just read have resonance across every project I touch? How can that person I just met bring value to one of my other contacts? As Raj told us, it's all about exploring the benefits of cross-pollination.

Name: Austin Kleon

Location: Austin, Texas

Twitter: @austinkleon

Twitter Bio: "I'm a writer who draws. Author of Steal Like An Artist and Newspaper Blackout.
Copywriter @Springboxist. http://austinkleon.com/about"

1   **So tell us your multidimensional talents, how you earn a living.** I still have a nine-to-five: I'm a copywriter at Springbox, an interactive marketing agency here in Austin.

I'm also a writer, artist, blogger and speaker. I've been blogging since 2005, and I wrote a book called *Newspaper Blackout* (Harper Perennial, 2010) and another book called *Steal Like an Artist* (Workman, 2012). I also sell fine art prints and speak at various events on creativity, visual thinking, and being an artist online.

This is the first year I made as much money off my art as I did at my day job – I always told myself, when I hit that point, I'd quit and do the art full time, but we'll see...

2   **When did you transition to go plural?** I grew up copying comics and making up stories with pictures and words – writing and drawing were always linked together. But once I got to school there was English class and Art class. Suddenly, writing and drawing were separate. I kept doing both, but when it came time for college I felt like I had to choose between art or literature. I thought literature was the more serious subject. I went over to England and studied at the University of Cambridge. I wrote perfectly adequate,

boring papers for my poor tutors, until one day I was doodling a map of Charles Dickens' *Our Mutual Friend* and decided to turn it in with my essay. My tutor said, 'This is better than any paper you've written.' So pretty much, from that point on, I've tried to keep pictures and words together in my life.

3   **What's your strategy for answering the 'What do you do?' dinner party/pub question?** I used to just say 'I'm a web designer' or 'I'm a copywriter' and leave out the art stuff. Now I just say 'I'm a writer' or 'I'm a writer and an artist' or 'I'm a writer who draws.'

4   **How do you sell your multidimensional talents?** My talents are basically a Venn diagram of pictures, words and the web, and that's usually my elevator pitch: I draw the Venn and say, 'I help folks tell stories with pictures and words on the web.'

5   **What are the joys of a work life where you mash up different talents?** It's never boring.

6   **And what are your pain points in doing more than one thing?** Finding work where you can integrate all those things – most of the time when you do several things you have to make your own work. And that can be painful.

HOW TO STAND OUT
FROM THE CROWD.

15

Mash-marketing

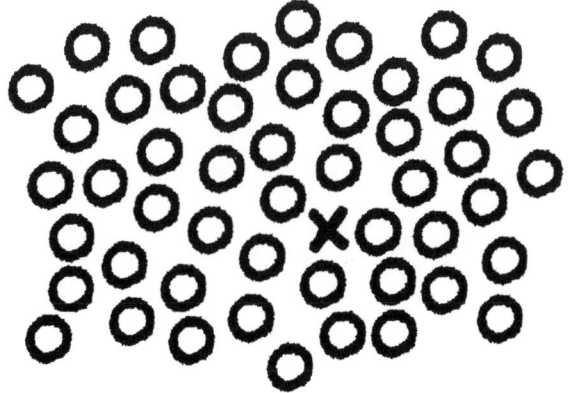

We saw in Chapter 9 the importance of your story in making you both distinctive and memorable. And we discovered in Chapter 4 how you discover your unifier. The unifier will most likely deliver your point of difference. In our abundant job market and business world, facing competition from every direction, similarly talented people pitching for the same jobs and opportunities, you have to stand out from the crowd. So once you've identified your point of difference – the unifier – you'll need to communicate that to the world. And with digital tools it's easier than ever.

▟▟ If you aren't different you have no identity. You're just a commodity... To have an identity you need a point of difference. And if you don't have one, you need to create one.

(Dave Trott, 2009)

So the point of difference is not just useful; it's essential. The brain is lazy on the grounds that it likes to be efficient and it takes a lot of calories for it to perform functions like decision making, so it prefers to group stuff together to make things simple for it. When you walk along a street your brain isn't recalling every make and model of car you pass; it just groups them all together as cars: simple. So for a car to get your attention it will need to stand out. For example, it may be a very old classic car, a ridiculously expensive sports car or simply a normal car but covered in dents, in which case you will be aware that the car has crashed into lots of things, and you will avoid it so that you are not next. All the rest of the cars will simply be grouped as 'category cars'. So when people meet you, and they will no doubt meet lots of people that day, how will you ensure they are able to place you in a category and how will you dominate the category they place you in so that you are first to be recalled when they need your skill? The bad news may be you've got stacks of competition out there; the good news is that your differentiator is unique and, what's more, online has given us a bunch of free tools to start spreading the word.

Let's start with your website. A website is a great way of communicating your plurality, making it simple via a home page communicating your unifier and, for instance, separate pages for each of your respective skills. That's relevant not just if you're a freelancer or self-employed; there is no reason why you can't have a personal website communicating your plurality when you work for an organization. Yes, David had a one-page website with links to his respective sites and social media feeds even though he could have easily felt that in his role as Executive Creative Director he didn't need to bother defining himself beyond that. So why bother? The power in the transparency of publishing a site clearly showing his multiple facets instantly made him more of an asset; clients could see the real and full value David could bring as a well-rounded bloke. They didn't see him just as his job title.

For people like the polymath broadcaster and writer Stephen Fry and the entrepreneur Martha Lane Fox, the personal website can provide great order and structure to that complexity. Making the complex simple makes what you do gettable, memorable, easy to grasp. The act of creating your website, highlighting your plurality in clear design and words, is powerful. It will reflect right back at you who you are and what you are not. If you feel uncomfortable with what you see then you can change it until it is a true reflection. The site map for Stephen's website at stephenfry.com is as comprehensive as that you might find for a global brand, with a very busy home page full of blog posts, news, links and social media feeds. But it remains gettable; you get an instant sense of all the different strings to his bow. Martha's site at marthalanefox.com is very ordered, with her different hats clearly communicated with logos for the different companies whose boards she serves on. Both sites manage to communicate not just the breadth of what Martha and Stephen do, but also what respectively makes them different.

Your website is that single – definitive – point of presence, providing a single shop window for displaying all your multiple wares. Shane Mac has a very stripped-down (but effective) site at shanemac.me with a list of every different hat he wears and passion he has (16 at the last count). You won't find any bells and whistles here, just a video of Shane and a list of all the different stuff he does with links. If you're struggling to create a simple website communicating all you do, why not steal a leaf out of Shane's book and try his approach? Simplicity wins.

Like your website, your presence on Twitter, Facebook or LinkedIn is there for all to see, all of the time. There can be no editing or pivoting to amplify one thing or another to fit the nuance of the audience. It puts the pressure on managing your identities online and getting your positioning exactly right.

Chris Poole, Founder of about.me and Canvas, gave a talk at Web 2.0 in 2011 where he said 'It's not who you share with; it's who you share as.' That really nailed it for us, because communicating your talents is about how the audience perceive you – it's less about who's checking you out on Twitter, and more what you're tweeting or how you're positioning yourself.

Twitter is a good natural storytelling platform, as it lets you share your multidimensional life. And that shouldn't be underestimated; indeed a potential client may discover more about you from following you on Twitter for a day than from reading your CV. They'll discover your interest in politics, your music tastes and your love of coffee. That gives a fuller picture than the snapshot offered by a CV.

What does your avatar say about you? Does your 140-character biography nail it? Look at your Twitter biography now and answer the question: how does it impact, communicate and persuade? It might be more important than your website or blog. Twitter is your at-a-glance platform, and it's incredibly important. When you follow someone on Twitter who you'd like to follow you back, you have a once-in-a-lifetime opportunity to get that person's attention. The person will make a snap judgement based on glancing at your Twitter biography. Being too cool, enigmatic or ambiguous does not work; it is unlikely that someone will spend time investigating whether you might be able to answer the kind of problems the person has; it is easier simply to move on. You will be followed or you will be unfollowed; what you say will make the difference.

And remember: your online profiles don't have to stand still. As your offering evolves and you add new strings to your bow, make sure you update your website and Twitter, LinkedIn and any other social media profiles. Do they carry the right message about you? Does it reflect your offering as it stands today? If not, change it.

As Phill Jupitus is probably best known in the UK as a panellist on the long-running BBC2 music show *Never Mind the Buzzcocks*, to most people he is just 'the bloke off the telly'. But the reality is that he has many, many more strings to his bow; as a profile in the *Guardian* newspaper said, he is 'not an easy guy to pigeonhole'. Over a couple of coffees, Phill told us his story and suggested that 'the thing that most people know you for becomes the shorthand for what you do'. He has actually found that a tool outside of his own control – Wikipedia – is responsible for communicating the true breadth of his talents beyond a single TV show. Phill told us:

> The only reason that people now know about all the different things I do is because of my Wikipedia page. If that Wikipedia page wasn't there people would go 'He's the guy off *Never Mind the Buzzcocks*, does a bit of stand-up.' They wouldn't know about any of the other stuff as well.

And here's what that Wikipedia entry says:

> Phillip Christopher Jupitus (born 25 June 1962) is an English stand-up and improvised comedian, actor, performance poet, musician and podcaster.
>
> (Wikipedia, 2012)

Of course, not all of us have the luxury of a Wikipedia page about us; that's why it's even more important that we get those other online touchpoints right, because there is no excuse not to bother. It is our problem – not our audience's – if they don't know everything we know. What do we mean by online 'touchpoints'? Just all those points online that touch your prospective audiences: from an e-mail footer to a website, a Google plus profile to LinkedIn, Facebook to Twitter.

Offline it can be easier, because we can be more chameleon-like, amplifying a talent, listening before responding. The entrepreneur, columnist and speaker Mike Southon told us his approach is to ask first: see what the person in front of him is interested in and then communicate accordingly. Mike has an alter ego; he's the frontman of a 70s tribute band, wearing a wig and sporting a ridiculous oversized moustache. That persona is a million miles away from Mike's reputation as a *Financial Times* columnist and public speaker. If the person he's just met is interested in music then he might mention the band, but for some people he won't mention it at all. He doesn't feel the need to be transparent – he can keep the two very separate.

On the other hand, when we spoke to Tom Hulme at IDEO, he told us how important transparency is to him. Because he has other business interests outside his day job, he thinks it's important that all parties know the full breadth of what he does, including the businesses he invests in and advises, so there is no conflict of interest. However, he does not wear a wig and sport a ridiculous moustache like Mike! Tom told us:

> I've always erred on the side of complete transparency. I'm very clear for instance on LinkedIn on listing the companies I've invested in, very deliberately because I don't want anyone to look back, at IDEO or at start-ups, and say 'I didn't know you were doing that.'

Effectively communicating your point of difference is more than just sticking to your unifier and shouting about it. It's about understanding the nuances of your audiences, the styles of the different platforms, the differences between Facebook and LinkedIn, and how your message needs to shift accordingly.

As Chris Poole said, it's not who you share with; it's who you share as.

Name: Frances Booth

Location: London

Twitter: @fran_booth

Twitter Bio: "Writer, photographer, skier.
http://www.herearesomewords.com"

1   **So tell us your multidimensional talents, how you earn
    a living.** I earn a living mainly from the 'writing, editing
    and training' side of my business. This all falls into the
    broad theme of 'words', and comes under my 'Here are
    some words' hat, herearesomewords.com.

    I added the 'Here are some pictures' side to
    my business in the summer of 2011, launching
    herearesomepictures.com. I'd been training and
    shooting to build up my skills for around two years
    before I launched my photography site. I'd been a keen
    photographer for many years, and as part of my job at
    telegraph.co.uk and guardian.co.uk selected pictures
    on a daily basis to publish on the web. I knew already
    I was a very visual person. When I write, I tend to use
    a lot of imagery.

2   **When did you transition to go plural?** I just decided
    that I wanted to go for it with pictures too – with the
    caveat that I wouldn't put too much financial pressure
    on it. I knew I could use 'words' to make a living while
    slowly building up 'pictures'. Photography is something
    I am massively passionate about, so it was a big deal
    to move it to a 'for the world to see' sphere. I saved up
    and set aside a month to fully focus on my photography
    – building and writing my site, attending photography
    events and generally immersing myself in it. I had a
    great reaction straight away, and soon after launching

was shortlisted for Outdoor Photographer of the Year. My two worlds – writing and photography – also linked up almost immediately.

3   What's your strategy for answering the 'What do you do?' dinner party/pub question? I try and find out about the person I'm talking to first, to see which element of my work (training, editing, writing, photography, well-being) will resonate with them. That then becomes the 'top line'.

4   How do you sell your multidimensional talents? Often I end up giving out two business cards, which I am sure seems slightly bizarre!

The sites do link to each other, but I don't want people to miss out on the bit they need. It's a bit tricky. There isn't really a business card or job title that covers the lot that people would comprehend. There is an overarching brand though, in 'Here are some [words/pictures]'. If I'm at a photography event, or a writing event, talking to photographers or writers, it's easier, and I'll mainly hand out just one type of card. Doing both writing and photography makes me a bit different (photographers don't tend to write much).

5   What are the joys of a work life where you mash up different talents? Launching the second strand, I knew so much more than the first time round. I was very clear straight away about my messaging and how I wanted my website to look – so much so that my second website ended up immediately way better than my first. While I still literally leapt up and down on the day the site was complete, it was a lot easier to just take a deep breath and launch. Second time around, it was a lot quicker and there was a lot less to work out. I'd been there and done it, so I just knew how to do it again.

6   **And what are your pain points in doing more than one thing?** One immediate downside was the realization I had to now go back and redo the 'words' website to make it as good as the photography one. I'm often torn as to what to spend time on. In a way, always having something else you want to do – whichever bit you're working on – keeps it all fresh. Often, I would love to while away the hours on my photography business, but I have to balance what is still a novelty and a 'luxury' with the day-to-day running and developing of the writing side of things, which is also at an exciting stage.

WELCOME TO MASHALYTICS – YOUR VERY OWN CUSTOMIZABLE DASHBOARD TO CONTROL EVERY ASPECT OF YOUR PLURAL LIFE.

16

Mashalytics

When you're busy working on multiple projects, wearing different hats, it can be easy to get so lost in what you're doing that you're not able to stand back from the day-to-day to check that what you're doing still matches your goal. You may have started producing doodles for clients as a side project because you're passionate about art, but haven't stopped to realize that the clients you're working with are no fun and have drained all your passion. How can you keep a handle on the different things you're doing, how they match your initial motivators and whether you are taking advantage of the interrelationships between them? Welcome to mashalytics – your very own customizable dashboard to control every aspect of your mashed-up life.

Creating your own dashboard is essential because, whilst you might have access to the constituent elements, it's completely different when you look at the overview. Your income might be telling you your career is paying well and you're making good money this month, but what's the point of it all if you know deep down you are not satisfied or stimulated because you find it so soul-destroying? You can't look at one piece of information in isolation; you have to look at it all together. The dashboard is powerful because it recognizes there is more than one metric, more than one measurable.

Just as the dials on a car dashboard show you how your engine is performing and warn you if you are about to run out of fuel, this one will tell you what is happening in your mashed working life. Think of it as your very own early warning system: the dashboard will give you warning when your time management is unbalanced, when you aren't earning enough money or when the inspiration fuel tank is low. That early warning will give you enough time to investigate the problem and make changes.

The dashboard will give you an indication so you know what action to take, what tweaks to make so your working life is sustainable both emotionally and financially. Being in control and informed, being able to see clearly how things are going, will better inform you to make clear decisions.

Now is the time to ask some important questions to establish if what you dreamt of is what you are actually doing. It's time to create your very own dashboard so you can gauge where you are.

Get out a piece of paper and a pen and let's plot out your dashboard. Why do we write it down? Because that makes it more powerful. Writing something down as it really is makes the facts hard to fudge (unlike carrying stuff around in your head) and serves as a helpful reminder of where you need to focus attention to move forward. Having it in black and white will mean you can't be in denial; you will have to address it, fix it, and then you can move forward. If you are not covering the bills then it may be time to make that the absolute focus of your attention and make suitable changes.

Start by listing all the things about your working life that are important: see our 10 suggestions below.

Draw around a coin to make your dial and then mark the needle position from a 1 to a 10, 1 being fatal and in need of immediate attention and 10 being excellent and no action required. Here are some ideas for 10 dials you can create:

1   **Emotional status:** How happy are you? Are you feeling satisfied with what you are doing?

2   **Income:** Are you making enough money? Are you charging enough for what you do?

3   **Client or employer satisfaction:** Is your client or boss pleased with what you're doing, seeing value in your contribution?

4   **Time management:** Are you working 18 hours a day? Do you need to be managing your time better?

5 **Inspiration fuel:** Are you feeding your soul, nourishing it with stimulus to be inspired so that you can do great work?

6 **Passion:** How is it scoring on passion? Are you loving what you are doing?

7 **People:** What are the people you are working with like? Not all clients and co-workers are good people to be around.

8 **Reputation:** How does what you're doing now add to your reputation? Is it something you can shout about?

9 **Marketing:** Are you making a noise about the stuff you are doing, and are you aiming that noise at the people who matter?

10 **Coming next:** Are you doing enough to ensure that you will have something to move on to? Nothing is permanent, and if you are not actively seeking your next gig then you should be.

On your dashboard, you now have in front of you a full view of all the things that matter. Feel free to add your own dial depending on your drivers and the nuances of your roles. This is your mashalytics tool. Use it to gently build your working life around passion, money, looking for new gigs and ensuring that you are maximizing on the potential to cross-pollinate.

Use these tools to manage your multidimensional life. Create a dashboard to make sure there is balance in your mash. Build your talents layer by layer, as you would with Lego. Make sure you're making the most of mashing: Are your passions being satisfied? Are you learning new ideas? How are you cross-pollinating ideas and contacts from one area to another? Make sure you take time to press the pause button and review all the mash on your plate...

Name: Mark Hillary

Location: São Paulo, Brazil

Twitter: @markhillary

Twitter Bio: "CEO of IT Decisions; British, based in São Paulo, Brazil. Write globalization/tech books, blog for Reuters & HuffPo, teach MBA, London 2012 Olympic storyteller! http://j.mp/markhillary"

1   **So tell us your multidimensional talents, how you earn a living.** If I have to sum up what I do, I just say 'writer', but being multidimensional that doesn't really start to describe it. I write books about technology and globalization, I write blogs for major news sites like *Reuters* and *Huffington Post* and help several companies with their blogs and social media use, I blog about technology in Brazil, I oversee a research company focused on the technology industry in Brazil, I speak at technology conferences all over the world, I teach MBA students at several universities, I advise the UN on technology in developing countries, and I have spent time working for the British government as a blogging mentor to schoolchildren.

2   **When did you transition to go plural?** I left my last regular job in 2002, so it is almost a decade now since I had a monthly pay cheque that I could rely on. While I was still in my job – I was a senior manager looking after technology for an investment bank – I had started contributing columns to a trade paper and became an industry commentator. By that point I had already written my first book, so I knew I could write.

I was enjoying the writing, doing more journalism, and I was getting disillusioned with the long-hours culture of banks in the City. On most days I was judged more for the hours I stayed in the office and number of flights I could take in a month rather than for any actual achievements. I wanted to move on to try something else, even though it would mean a dramatic drop in income.

3   What's your strategy for answering the 'What do you do?' dinner party/pub question?
I usually start by saying I'm a writer of books and blogs, but if we end up talking for a while then the poor person who can describe their working life in a single word – accountant, lawyer, manager – usually ends up bamboozled by the array of different areas and activities I get involved with. 'Writer' keeps it simple, but even that's not foolproof, as most people associate the word writer with novelist (perhaps I should write a novel?).

4   How do you sell your multidimensional talents?
Mostly through media activity: writing in the media, producing new books, being seen as a commentator on subjects like the convergence of technology, globalization and politics. I get enquiries from people because of these activities and also because of conference talks, where I give advice, but often companies will ask me to help them on a more individual basis. Sometimes the promotional activity has to be done for nothing – a lot of media contributors do give their expertise for nothing these days because it positions them well for following up their media profile with corporate work.

5 **What are the joys of a work life where you mash up different talents?** The joy is in having a lot of control in how to spend my time. I can be flexible in my working hours and, with a lot of different activities, if someone annoys me then I won't work with them again. I have enough work to be able to ditch the painful contracts. Getting paid to travel to interesting places is also another great benefit, though in my early banking career I did do a great deal of international travel to the point at which I was entirely jaded – now I aim for something more like a trip a month, so I have my base, but I can still get out into the world to see what is going on and to comment on it.

6 **And what are your pain points in doing more than one thing?** Prioritization is important and can be difficult. Sometimes the really fun things are the ones that don't earn you any money, and there may be some promotional justification in doing them, but not at the expense of not delivering on a piece of client work that has a deadline. So this kind of life needs a lot of juggling and an acceptance that, even though this is better than working nine to five in the same office every day, there are still times when a client wants you to do something that is not really fun.

WHY STAYING AGILE
AND ALLOWING
OPPORTUNITIES TO COME TO
FRUITION VIA SERENDIPITY
ARE MORE POWERFUL THAN
A CAREER PLAN.

17

How to unplan for success

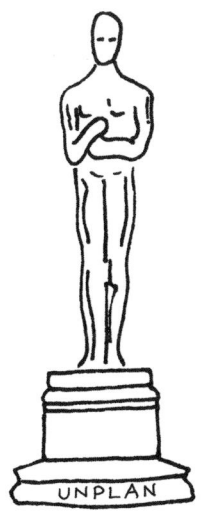

You might think to start your plural work life you will need a clear plan, a map that shows you where you are going to end up and exactly how you will get there. We disagree. When we think of plans they tend to be complex and contain pie charts and projections that require to be compiled by analysts. Is this what you really need to do to go plural? No. Most plans are rubbish, written by people who are guessing the future based on what has happened in the past. The past is exactly that, the past; it has gone, and even though it has a habit of repeating it can't be used as an absolute map for the future.

Comedian Phill Jupitus agrees: he likes his career to be organic:

❝ **It's never been about a plan and it never will be. As soon as you start having a plan, [it goes wrong].**

So success at mashing is about staying open to possibilities, doing a career slalom embracing what we have billed 'the unplan'. What is the unplan? Well, it's a philosophy both of us have embraced for years, that we don't have a grand strategy for our next career move, our next project or our next book. Instead we rely on our instinct, on seeing where the water flows, spotting opportunities and going for them. For us, that philosophy is at the heart of mashing, staying agile to add new strings to our bow, allowing opportunities to come to fruition via serendipity.

Why do people feel compelled to have their personal career plan? If you want to be singular in your career then you can climb a ladder, and a plan guiding you on that journey might help. You can see where you are, where you want to go next and what the journey will look like. If you're starting out as a lawyer and want to stay in law your whole career, a 10-year career plan may make sense. But in a plural world where you elect to stay agile and open-minded to opportunities, by its very nature, there can be no fixed plan.

However, whilst a carefully plotted career plan may be meaningless, we all recognize the value of having a goal in mind, ie something we want to achieve. So we like goals (in fact we love them); it's just that we don't like carefully plotted linear routes to get there. So have that goal, or those goals. I will write a book. That deal will come off. I will launch my side project website. Visualize that meeting; visualize seeing your book on the shelf; see yourself shaking hands on the new deal. But acknowledge the contribution of *luck*. Many people's success stories owe a lot to randomness and serendipity, and no plan can anticipate those. Ask people their reason for career success and many reply 'It's all happened by accident.'

Not having a plan means you are always ready to embrace change or to react rapidly and smartly to new projects, client or employer needs that you can fill, or the possibilities that can be provided by technological change. A plan can end up being the obstacle to just getting on and doing it. When it comes to adding a new string to your bow, you may think you need to plan for that, rather than dive straight in. But it's often more effective to try it, to see if you can do it, if you like doing it, and if you can get people paying for it.

In the absence of plans to help make decisions in your career, what tools does every masher need to turn the dreams into reality? Adding a new string to your bow can be frightening; it takes guts. The best tool you can use? Your instinct. To take that risk and go with your gut feeling. When you're asking what shape your side project takes, what your personal website looks like, how much to charge for that hobby project – certainly, ask your friends, co-workers and clients. But at the end of the day you have the answer inside. You just have to trust your gut feeling. Go with it every time.

Being reactionary is not about being weak or unfocused. It's about being ready for action, ready to react to situations to take advantage of opportunities that land in your lap... just like that. It's having the right attitude to spot an opportunity and go for it, to adapt to changing economic, technological and market changes. With a rigid fixed-plan mindset, that's difficult. Keeping flexible and open-minded is the way to succeed, or you could miss out on some great career opportunities.

Follow up that random meeting in a café. Stop and have a chat with the person standing next to you in a queue and don't be afraid to ask lots of questions about something you don't quite understand. Planning is just a little overrated in our opinion, and too many times we have worked with disappointed people whose plans fell short.

Tom Hulme, Design Director at IDEO, told us:

❝❝ The best opportunities come unplanned; they come serendipitously.

Tom confessed that none of the ideas he's had are that unique, but he acknowledges he ensures he's fast at spotting opportunities and then acting quickly:

So I've been lucky repeatedly, but I've done my best to put myself in a position where I can capitalize on that luck.

Of course, by its very nature, it's difficult to strategize for luck or serendipity, but to be an effective masher you need to stay open-minded to new opportunities and then prepared to act fast.

Simply put, you will be faced with uncertainty, and plans aren't very good at accommodating uncertainty. In the fast-moving world where we find ourselves, where new opportunities arise suddenly and randomly, such plans are meaningless. Embracing the spirit of unplan is not about being lazy or being sloppy. It's about being goal focused and having the right attitude for success. It's about going for it, not just talking about it.

Name: Shane Mac

Location: Seattle

Twitter: @ShaneMac

Twitter Bio: "Just some dude. Product @zaarly. Founded @sayhellothere. Was at Gist and Cobalt, both acquired. Click the link. http://shanemac.me/"

1   **So tell us your multidimensional talents, how you earn a living.** I lead product at a start-up called Zaarly. I also have a side company, Hello There (sayhellothere.com). I'm a professional musician and play shows when I have extra time. I've also written a book, *Stop with the BS.*

2   **When did you transition to go plural?** I started out playing music and accidentally got into technology after I had to market and promote all of my shows and create a website... That was eight years ago. I loved technology and creating experiences that brought everyone together and made the world a more connected place.

3   **What's your strategy for answering the 'What do you do?' dinner party/pub question?** I think in hierarchy. Zaarly is first. I have a team that counts on me, and we are going after changing how the economy works, not a small vision. If the conversation leads to other things then I just discuss things that may be of interest to that group or could benefit others from something that I've done – music, digital marketing, a book or even starting a three-person side product.

4   How do you sell your multidimensional talents?
I really don't. I try to excel and be good at one thing at a given point in time. Perfect it and then you will always have it. Sometimes you'll have to touch up your skills, but usually if you focus on being really good at one thing people will notice. Over time, those one things stack up and become many. I think trying to do a ton of things at one time is the recipe for disaster.

5   What are the joys of a work life where you mash up different talents? Music has taught me a lot about bringing an entire room of people together to feel like a part of a greater movement. I think that is what drives me. What happens when you make an entire venue sing the words to a song, regardless of gender, age or race, is the same thing that happens when you create a clear vision and bring a team together.

6   And what are your pain points in doing more than one thing? Sometimes I wonder if the things that come after my main priority could be bigger and have a great impact on the world.

WHY THE FUTURE IS IN
FLUX – AND WHAT YOU CAN
(AND CAN'T) DO ABOUT IT.

18

Workflux

So – of course – the future is uncertain (that is why you need your unplan). There's been an unprecedented amount of change in the last five years, economic, political and commercial – so much so that no one can give you an accurate answer to the 'What's next?' question. We really have no idea what is around the corner, what economic calamity will slam into us and force us to rethink our business and career, what political change may derail the nation's confidence or how our impact on our environment will manifest itself. Big questions that demand big answers, yet every time another hero claims to have the solution they seem to get knocked out quickly, their plans dashed by an unexpected left hook. So we are left to consider this: big plans, long-range forecasting and predictions are for foolish optimists who believe that it will be like it was before. It will not. Uncertainty reigns supreme. Those who adopt an agile mindset, who can do more than one thing and be adaptable and enterprising, stand the best chance of success.

At the heart of this uncertainty, new business models, products and innovations are shaking up not just how business is done but also how we perform our roles. Mashing those roles together effectively will require a certain mindset, what Robert Safian, Editor of *Fast Company*, has billed 'Generation Flux':

▌▌ Because some people will thrive. They are the members of Generation Flux. This is less a demographic designation than a psychographic one: What defines GenFlux is a mind-set that embraces instability, that tolerates – and even enjoys – recalibrating careers, business models, and assumptions. Not everyone will join Generation Flux, but to be successful, businesses and individuals will have to work at it.

(Safian, 2012)

This is an era when the most important skill is the ability to acquire new ones. So how are you scoring on that front? DJ Patil is a GenFluxer. His LinkedIn profile promises 'Diverse experiences in a wide range of domains' before listing an eye-watering list of specialities from risk management to data mining. With experience working in academia, in government, in big public companies and in start-ups as both a technologist and an entrepreneur, he is hard to define. Who knows what he will be or do next? 'That doesn't bother me', he says. 'I'll find something' (Safian, 2012). Those who demonstrate elasticity will have greater potential to succeed in this uncharted world, whilst everyone in what they might think is a 'stable job' will need to answer the question 'What's next?', ready to open their toolbox to offer multiple tools and skills to the job market for their next position. Doing the same job at a similar company just won't be an option any more.

A mindset for success relies on not just agility but remaining fluid enough to explore new opportunities with no great agenda. Tom Hulme wasn't recruited by IDEO for any of the things he actually spends most of his time doing, but the organization embraces the fact that he's pushed into new areas, such as building a separate, stand-alone business. The organization gave Tom permission to explore and it's paid off. Tom said:

> I have permission at IDEO to take my career in almost any direction. I've earned trust. People trust if I go off piste it might be an interesting and valuable place to go.

In this state of flux there can be no 5- or 10-year career plan, climbing a ladder at a corporation in the hope that if you work hard enough and keep your head down you'll be rewarded with a promotion and a pay rise in the next 12 months. Those were the old ways in the old days. In this new uncharted world, it's about embracing your curiosity, exploring new avenues and taking random left turns. Your best strategy is to use your instinct to navigate where you go next.

So what does your future look like? If you can see only three months ahead, then deal with that and enjoy the certainty of those three months, whilst not getting hung up on trying to forecast beyond. Don't try to guess what's beyond, but be open to observing what's around you and how that can fit in today and beyond. Try to view that blank canvas as exactly that: not a chasm of uncertainty, but a canvas on which to paint your future.

Today, set in motion the mindset and actions that will start making new opportunities real. If you run the business, try asking your staff if they have any ideas how they can grow their role and redefine it, reshape it and rename it. If you're your own boss, ask yourself how you can add more value to your clients and their business. If you work for yourself, ask what string you'll add to your bow next. What additional skill could you sell an existing client? Can you develop a new service to react to a client need? Remember that opportunities aren't always going to land in your lap, so you will need to take the initiative to create the work life that reflects your own talents and aspirations. In this scrambled-up world, you can do U-turns, take detours and reinvent your offering as you see fit. As we write these words in February 2012, neither of us has a fixed plan for the next 12 months. We each have a number of projects, roles and ventures we are exploring. Experience has shown us that it's futile trying to look too far into the future. Instead, have aspirations, head towards them and take time often to lift up your head and observe where you have come from, where you are going and where you want to be next. Do not delude yourself; face the harsh reality that things will change, and where necessary make that change yourself.

The only known truth for us is that our futures are plural not singular; both of us are creating work lives full of interesting multiple projects, consisting of stuff that stimulates us, things that pay our bills, things that get us out of our beds in the morning, things we'll be proud to tell our grandkids in years to come.

So this is it: this is how things can be. You just need the courage to start creating your new working life, to go plural. Whether you're going to go in to work tomorrow and ask your boss if she'll give you the autonomy to carve out your own role or whether you're going to use your talent as a foundation to which you're going to add new skills on top, it's time to start doing it. Start that blog; volunteer for that community gardening project; say you'll manage the company Twitter account; let that client know you can advise them on a bunch of other stuff as well. And the good news is you don't need a grand plan; you just need to stay open-minded and flexible about what the opportunities are and go with the flow.

> **What we really want to do is what we are really meant to do. When we do what we are meant to do, money comes to us, doors open for us, we feel useful, and the work we do feels like play to us.**
> (Julia Cameron, The Artist's Way, 2011)

From bars to boardrooms, we're hearing the same message. The future is about *projects*. Whether it's setting up that web-based business on the side, adding another string to your bow at the office or spotting a niche you can fill, the future is about mashing up multiple interests and talents so you can deliver on projects. The future is not about doing one thing; it's about doing many things. That's of no surprise to the freelancer, but to the rest of us in day jobs and to companies employing staff it may take some getting used to. It's time to forget the old way of career ladders, being a specialist in a single discipline all your life, and open your mind to a plural work life. Start embracing doing what you love, mashing roles together, crossing borders and cross-pollinating completely different disciplines.

Name: Stephanie Booth

Location: Lausanne, Switzerland

Twitter: @stephtara

Twitter Bio: "Anglo-Swiss. Blogger-speaker-trainer-consultant-geek. Works at @eclau. Tries to sing and sail at times, and misses her Indian cat @bagha. http://climbtothestars.org"

1   **So tell us your multidimensional talents, how you earn a living.** My talents have to do with the web and social media, but inside there they are pretty scattered. I do speaking engagements, training and consulting. I'm the editor for a couple of blogs. I run a co-working space. I direct a year-long course on social media in Lausanne. I manage blogger accreditations for the conference LeWeb in Paris.

Aside from that, I've had various 'areas of expertise' over the years: teenagers and the internet; multilingualism online; corporate blogging, when it was young; blogging; blogger relations; freelancing (I organized a conference on the topic in 2008, Going Solo); co-working. I'm also pretty geeky (I've written plug-ins for WordPress and understand pretty much how a server works), but good with words and more 'human' stuff – a combination not everybody expects.

2   **When did you transition to go plural?** I'm not sure I transitioned. Even when I was still in school, I signed up to go into a special class (labelled 'X') to do both arts and science. I've always had very diverse interests. I started studying chemistry, failed, and then went into arts. While I was finishing my degree in history of religions, I was working in the world of business, for a large local company.

If I have to point out a transition, it will be when I went freelance. From 2004 to 2006 I was a schoolteacher. Early 2005, the local press started taking an interest in my blogging (I'd been blogging since 2000) and what I had to say. People asked me to teach them how to make websites. I started giving talks in other schools. I did some consulting for a start-up (community management before it was hip). My freelance activity grew out of these various bits and pieces I was doing aside from my day job. It was a natural transition.

3   **What's your strategy for answering the 'What do you do?' dinner party/pub question?** I wince. Well, for many years I winced. My business cards have gone through a variety of incarnations. It started with 'blogging consultant' back in the day, when that was all it was. I've always held back from using something like 'social media consultant', because it means everything and nothing.

Nowadays, I say this: 'Well, my job had to do with social media – you know, Facebook, Twitter, blogs and the like. I help people and companies understand what all this stuff is, and then figure out what's useful in there for them and what isn't. Concretely, I give talks, train people, do short-term consulting, and sometimes end up working on projects for my clients. Right now I'm the editor for a couple of blogs; I co-direct a course on social media; I manage blogger accreditations for a conference. I also run a co-working space. That kind of stuff.'

It's not exactly short. Depending on the context I'll stop after the first sentence. Or the second. Or go on to explain more if the person in front of me is curious.

4   How do you sell your multidimensional talents?
I don't really, to be honest. I probably need to get better
at that – I've been in situations where, because I was
hired for certain parts of my expertise, other aspects
of it tended to be dismissed by some of the people
I interacted with. What I do is just run people through
what I do and can do, depending on what they're
asking, or what I think may be useful to them.

**5   What are the joys of a work life where you mash up
different talents?** For me, clearly, variety, and being
who I am. I am a very multidimensional person.
Combining expertise in areas people don't expect to be
compatible is something I like a lot about myself.

**6   And what are your pain points in doing more than one
thing?** Feeling scattered. And in a market that's
catching up with 'pioneer me', the stress of realizing
that I cannot keep up in all my areas of activity if I want
to remain competitive. I feel that I'm regrouping
(around my first love, blogging). But the point in doing
this is also to rationalize the 'money-earning' part of my
job to free up space to tinker, read more, write more,
do other things. Another pain point is the difficulty in
explaining what I do, even though, after five years or
so of doing it, I've found a way of dealing with that
which I'm quite happy about. Yet another is the feeling
that, as I have expertise in various domains, I can't
compete with those who do 'only that'.

TOOLS 'N' TIPS TO MANAGE YOUR MASH-UP LIFE

19

The mashifesto

1 **Think plural:** Don't shy away from doing more than one thing; embrace all your natural talents.

2 **Do it on the side:** If you think you're too busy in your nine-to-five to explore plurality, then start a side project in your spare time.

3 **Time is a precious commodity:** Manage it well; don't waste time on stuff that doesn't add value to your goal.

4 **Embrace the unplan:** Have career and business goals but don't have a fixed plan to get there.

5 **Fire up your mashalytics:** Make sure you're reviewing your mashed-up life.

6 **Put your desk on wheels:** If you're finding that your office or desk is not conducive to getting results, try working from new or different spaces. The library or coffee shops are a good start.

7 **Celebrate your weirdness:** You are your story, so don't shy away from those interesting bits in your back story that make you different.

8 **Be a good storyteller:** You need to compete on your story and use digital tools to tell that online.

9 **1+1 = 3:** Consider the collective power of your mashing, and how the respective strings to your bow can cross borders to add value elsewhere.

10 **Be curious:** Explore your curiosity to add more strings to your bow.

References

Boches, Edward (2011) The most important job in advertising, *Creativity Unbound* blog, 12 May

Brown, Tim (2007) Strategy by design, *Fast Company*, 19 December

Cameron, Julia (2011) *The Artist's Way: A spiritual path to higher creativity*, Pan, London

Cook, Jake (n.d.a) Facebook's Ben Barry on how to hack your job, *the99percent.com*

Cook, Jake (n.d.b) Hillman Curtis: on reinvention and taking the courageous path, *the99percent.com*

Hardy, Steve (2005) The creative generalist: how broad thinking leads to big ideas, *ChangeThis.com*, http://changethis.com/manifesto/19.CreativeGeneralist/pdf/19.CreativeGeneralist.pdf

Hiemstra, Glen (2011) The future of jobs, *Futurist.com*, 3 June

Isaacson, Walter (2011) *Steve Jobs*, Simon & Schuster, New York

MacLeod, Hugh (2009) *Ignore Everybody: And 39 other keys to creativity*, Portfolio, London

Malbon, Ben (2010) Presentation, 7 June, http://www.slideshare.net/benmalbon/are-you-ready-to-form-voltron-june-2010

Merchant, Nilofer (2011) And who are you?,
Yes and Know blog, 24 August

Pansolini, Cristina (2012) My first year: Saatchi &
Saatchi NY, *Advertising Week* blog, 10 January

Raje, Aparna Piramal (2011) Global
micro-entrepreneur, *livemint.com*, 23 October

Safian, Robert (2012) Generation Flux,
Fast Company, February

Trott, Dave (2009) *Creative Mischief*,
LOAF Marketing, London

Index

Index